KU-033-526

To Dad –
Enjoy!
Love from
Emma x

LORD'S

THE CATHEDRAL OF CRICKET

STEPHEN GREEN

LORD'S
THE CATHEDRAL OF CRICKET

TEMPUS

FOR MY SISTER ROSEMARY

First published 2003

Tempus Publishing Limited
The Mill, Brimscombe Port,
Stroud, Gloucestershire, GL5 2QG

© Stephen Green, 2003

The right of Stephen Green to be identified as the Author
of this work has been asserted in accordance with the
Copyrights, Designs and Patents Act 1988.

All rights reserved. No part of this book may be reprinted
or reproduced or utilised in any form or by any electronic,
mechanical or other means, now known or hereafter invented,
including photocopying and recording, or in any information
storage or retrieval system, without the permission in writing
from the Publishers.

British Library Cataloguing in Publication Data.
A catalogue record for this book is available from the British Library.

ISBN 0 7524 2167 0

Typesetting and origination by Tempus Publishing Limited.
Printed and bound in Spain.

CONTENTS

Stephen Green is a Lord's phenomenon, or at least he is as I write this foreword. He will soon pass into MCC legend and become an ex-phenomenon for he retires from his post as MCC's curator at the end of September 2003. On the same day, I step down from the Presidency of MCC. However I will have been in my post for a mere twelve months whereas Stephen has been the great club's Curator and Librarian for 35 years.

In those 35 years he has given tremendous service to the MCC Museum and Library, overseeing the acquisition of much momentous cricketing memorabilia and taking care of many, many more, from the Ashes downwards. He leaves the Museum at Lord's in magnificent shape, a shrine to the game he loves, an artistic and historical accumulation unmatched in the world of cricket, if not in the whole of sport. Many a visitor has come to Lord's for a day's cricket and has been unexpectedly grateful for bad weather – because of which he or she has discovered the Museum, where rain never stops play, where there are always great England cricketers to admire, where the past becomes the present, where the sun never sets on the best game of all.

No one more appropriate than Stephen could write a complete history of his most famous workplace. Although not there right at the start, he has been in the saddle for over 16 per cent of the lifetime of Lord's ground, as Presidents, Chairmen, Club Secretaries and Committees have come and gone. I am fortunate that it has fallen to me in my Presidential Year to write a few sentences about S.E.A. Green and *Lord's: The Cathedral of Cricket*, but I know that all of my predecessors since Stephen first made his mark here would have burst into print with equal enthusiasm about his entertaining and learned tome.

Sir Tim Rice
President, MCC
August 2003

The reopening of the MCC Museum by the Prime Minister, the Rt Hon John Major, on 19 May 1993. From left to right: Barry Mazur (Museum designer), John Major, Stephen Green, Michael Sissons (the Chairman MCC Arts and Library Committee).

INTRODUCTION

It was, I think, the late and great Sir Robert Menzies who first coined the phrase that Lord's was the cathedral of cricket. I am grateful to the publishers of this book for deciphering my handwriting correctly. This does not always happen. A friend of mine who is a distinguished writer has handwriting which is only marginally better than mine. His publishers could not read what he had written and said that Lord's was the Caterham of cricket. It is not intended to be disrespectful of that great and historic centre of cricket in Surrey to say that this was not what he had in mind.

I had never been to Lord's before I was summoned to my interview in 1968. I was lucky in that one of my interrogators was Desmond Eagar, who had been educated at my old college. Even more fortunately, I was wearing a Hampshire tie. Desmond was Secretary of that great county. The chairman of the interview panel was Lt-Gen. Sir Oliver Leese. In due course, he was to become my friend and mentor and I still think one of two nicest people I have ever met.

I have been extremely lucky in the Chairmen of the MCC Arts and Library Sub-Committee. Where but Lord's could one have known the following office holders? My chairmen were, in chronological order, the former commander of the Eighth Army, a director of the Bank of England, the doyen of cricket writers, a (possibly *the*) leading literary agent, the chairman of a world-famous auction house, the former Chairman of the Bar Council and the former Private Secretary to Her Majesty the Queen.

Through Lord's I have known a former Prime Minister and a retired Archbishop of Canterbury, but it is not only the great and the good that come to mind. Large numbers of so-called 'ordinary' people have crossed my path and in some cases become my friends. There is indeed more to Lord's than just cricket.

I have often had occasion to tell people that Lord's has been part of the London scene for considerably longer than has Trafalgar Square. MCC is one of the very oldest clubs in London of any description. It is necessary to remind our many visitors from the Antipodes that MCC was founded in 1787. European settlement of Australia did not begin in earnest until 1788…

It would need an abler pen than I possess to describe in great detail the full story of Lord's over the past 215 years. What I have tried to do has been to write an extended essay giving a popular, but (I hope) accurate account of what I regard as some of the more significant events in the club's history. It is perhaps surprising that there are cricket lovers who do not know how Lord's received its name. Others think that MCC has something to do with Middlesex; I have even heard a distinguished public figure the other day think it stood for the Metropolitan Cricket Club. Quite a few people are also unaware that there have been three grounds which have borne the noble name of Lord's.

After 35 years it is time to draw stumps and hand over to my able successor. I have always relished those days when Lord's has almost been synonymous with England itself – those moments when the weather forecasters make a special mention of what the elements are going to get up to in St John's Wood.

Over the years Lord's has witnessed many events. These have involved military parades at the time of the

Tossing for Innings by Robert James, *c.* 1841.

Napoleonic Wars, balloon ascents, athletic races, an encampment by Native Americans, surveying exercises by Sir George Everest, the drawing up of experimental rules for the new game of lawn tennis, railway tunnelling, bomb disposal, doodlebug adventures, bomb scares, streakers and political protest. Through all this the noble game of cricket has been played – even if no less a person than Mr Gladstone tried to stop a Secretary of MCC from taking a team to North America.

For many years this was a predominantly male world. Happily, in recent times, women's cricket has become much more prominent. Lord's has for a long time had an international membership – there were, for instance, Indian members of MCC back in the reign of Queen Victoria. The famous 'egg and bacon' tie has proved a passport to finding good friends and generous hospitality throughout the cricketing world.

At its best, Lord's has always stood for what is finest in our national life. MCC has been the guardian of the laws of cricket for over two centuries and its mission remains what it has always been – namely, to uphold the spirit of the game. Long may this continue.

Stephen Green
Lord's
August 2003

Underneath the arches: the Mound Stand. (Photograph by James Finlay.)

one

1787 – 1814

BEGINNINGS

An Exact Representation of the Game of Cricket, L.P. Boitard (1737-1763).

For at least a quarter of a millennium, cricket has been played in the St Marylebone district of north-west London. The famous and informative portrayal *Cricket in the Marylebone Fields* was painted in 1748. The artist was Francis Hayman, who was to become a founder member of the Royal Academy twenty years later. Hayman's depiction of a game in what is now known as Regent's Park is probably the most famous of all early cricket paintings and it deservedly holds pride of place in the Long Room at Lord's.

The picture gives a splendid idea of what cricket must have looked like in the middle of the eighteenth century – including curved bats, two-stump wickets and scorers notching up the runs on their tally sticks, together with underarm bowling and umpires standing near the wickets holding their bats. Looking at Hayman's work, one can easily discern a complete absence of any protective clothing. There are those who say that this painting does not in fact represent a specific locality. The jury may still be out on this issue, but we do know for certain that cricket was being played in the Marylebone area around that time. The *Daily Advertiser* provides early evidence for this state of affairs in, for example, the edition of 31 August 1752. This paper recorded that a match was due to be played on that day between the Marylebone Club and all of London. The prize was to be a guinea a man.

In the second half of the eighteenth century, however, the cricketing scene shifts away from the capital. The story moves from London to the little Hampshire village of Hambledon. This delightful place is, even to this day, a little off the beaten track and 250 years ago it must have seemed very remote indeed. This hallowed site in the development of our national game has been called the cradle (but not the birthplace) of cricket. It was here that teams from the area around this rustic ground could take on, and moreover defeat, sides which had been drawn from all over the South of England.

The patron of the Hambledon Club in 1787 was George Finch, the 9th Earl of Winchilsea. It is of interest,

incidentally, to note that on 14 July 1789 (the day of the storming of the Bastille) Lord Winchilsea was busy playing cricket at Hambledon in the match between Hampshire and Kent. Lord Winchilsea was educated at Eton College and at Christ Church, Oxford. In 1989 MCC was able to purchase a fine portrait of him, for which he had posed when studying at the latter institution. In this striking painting, Lord Winchilsea is depicted as a Nobleman Commoner. The artist was the well-known painter Nathaniel Dance, who himself had cricketing connections.

Apart from Hambledon, Lord Winchilsea's other Mecca was the White Conduit Cricket Club in Islington. This place was the leading centre of the game in the metropolis at that time. It was here that Lord Winchilsea was to meet an interesting young man who came from a very different social background and who hailed from the other end of

A song about the game of cricket, published by the Hambledon Club.

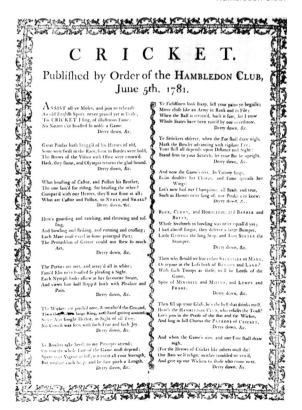

Cricket in the Marylebone Fields by Francis Hayman, *c.*1748.

John Nyren, pictured in 1805. Nyren was the author of a famous cricket book *The Cricketers of My Time*. His father ran the Bat & Ball Inn and the pair of them were instrumental in the running of the Hambledon Club.

The Bat & Ball Inn, Hambledon.

England. This cricketer was named Thomas Lord and he originated from the Yorkshire market town of Thirsk. The White Conduit Cricket Club drew many of its players from the patrons of the Star & Garter Inn, which was situated in Pall Mall. In the 1780s, some members of the Star & Garter began to play cricket on the White Conduit Fields. It was here that the young Thomas Lord was to make his cricketing debut as a ground bowler and as a general factotum.

'Thomas, son of William Lord, labourer, born November 23rd 1755. Baptised 29th December 1755.' This somewhat concise entry is to be found in the parish records of Thirsk. Behind these rather laconic words, however, one can discover an interesting story. The Lord family are believed to have experienced considerable prosperity in former days but they are understood at a later date to have fallen on hard times. The romantic legend would have us believe that some members of the Lord family were Roman Catholics who had given support – whether active or tacit is unclear – to the Jacobite cause and as a result of this disloyal behaviour had been deprived of their land. While it is certain that Bonnie Prince Charlie came through the North of England as far south as Derby in 1745, there is, alas, no firm evidence to support any involvement on the part of the Lord family in the Jacobite cause.

Thomas Lord was clearly a very ambitious man who would not be content to stay for long in what must then have seemed to be a provincial backwater. He had no prospects where he was situated and therefore decided to make a move, first to the Norfolk town of Diss and from there to London. After arriving in the capital he soon made his mark and in the course of time became a very successful wine merchant in the St Marylebone area. If he was not a member already, he must at some early stage in his career have joined the Church of England, because we know from the records that in 1807 he became a member of the St Marylebone Vestry. This was a position akin to being a member of the Town Council today.

Cricket, however, was his first love. It was at the White Conduit Club that he would have been introduced to several of the notables of the day, including Lord Winchilsea and Charles Lennox (who was later to become the 4th Duke of Richmond). The former in particular was very keen that Lord should set about founding a more central cricket club in Marylebone and that he should feel free to call the ground after his own name. In addition, Lord Winchilsea arranged that the young Yorkshireman should be indemnified against any possible financial loss that he might incur in setting up or continuing this momentous cricketing venture.

Thomas Lord soon got to work and he obtained a lease on part of the Portman family's estates in what was in those days known as Dorset Fields. A smaller part of this area (which today lies roughly between Baker Street and Marylebone stations) is nowadays to be found in the present Dorset Square. On 31 May 1787 the memorable day dawned on which Middlesex (with two of Berkshire and one of Kent) played against Essex (with two given men) for 100 guineas. Middlesex were the eventual winners in this historic encounter by a margin of 93 runs.

When MCC reached its bicentenary in 1987, attempts were made in some quarters to dispute the date, which has always traditionally been given for the foundation of the club. There is, however, in the MCC collection an engraving that was made in 1837 to celebrate the Golden Jubilee of Lord's. The inscription round the margin of this print (which was made to record the match between North and South that year) specifically states that the game was held to commemorate the fiftieth year of the Marylebone Club. The contemporary record is thus very clear; moreover, people would have been alive at the time that could have contradicted it if the information had been inaccurate.

George, 9th Earl of Winchilsea, painted by Nathaniel Dance (1734-1811) in 1771. This fine portrait depicts the man described by Sir Pelham Warner as 'the founder of MCC' when he was an undergraduate at Christ Church, Oxford. The painting was purchased by MCC in 1989.

Handkerchief depicting cricket at the White Conduit Fields, Islington.

The famous portrait of Thomas Lord. The painting was donated to
MCC by his last surviving descendant, Miss Florence Lord, in 1930.

Furthermore, the very first words of the earliest surviving MCC minute book state categorically: 'The Marylebone Club was established at Lord's Ground in the year 1787.' This was quite clearly a definite move to put the record straight for all time after a devastating fire, which took place in 1825, had destroyed all the early records of the club.

Because of this disastrous conflagration, we cannot know with total certainty the names of the early members of MCC. In the papers of the Finch family (to which Lord Winchilsea belonged) there is, however, a clue. These archives are deposited in the County Record Office for Leicestershire. Among these documents one can see a copy of the Laws of Cricket as revised at the Star & Garter in 1784. If one looks at the wording at the foot of these laws, one can read a list of members of the cricket club. It is a very reasonable assumption that most of these names will have shortly afterwards become founder members of the MCC. In addition, there is preserved among the Finch papers one of the famous volumes of scores compiled by Samuel Britcher. He was the original scorer at Lord's – in 2003 MCC reprinted his scorebooks in a limited edition.

In addition to the portrait of Lord Winchilsea, which MCC was able to buy in 1989, there is a fine likeness of him at the Royal Institution in Albermarle Street, which he helped to found. The MCC painting is dated 1771 – sixteen years before the sitter was to meet Thomas Lord. In between posing for the portrait and becoming the founding father of MCC, Lord Winchilsea had had a very eventful life, including taking part in the American War of Independence.

As a consequence of the fire in 1825 it was thought until recently that there were no documents extant linking Thomas Lord with cricket, although there are papers in existence which are connected with his civic duties. In the bicentenary year of MCC in 1987, however, the County Archivist at the North Yorkshire Record Office in Northallerton found a receipt written on a small scrap of paper. This read 'Recd June 15 1793 of Ld Mulgrave Two Guineas for his sub to the Cricket Club for the year 1792.

£2-2-0. Thos Lord'. Unlike the situation which prevails today, Lord Mulgrave would appear to have been given nearly eighteen months' grace to pay his subscription. On the other hand, two guineas represented rather a large sum – by comparison, today's subscription rates seem to represent extremely good value for money.

On 1 July 1793, the *Sporting Magazine* published an illustration of a 'Grand Match played in Lord's Ground, Marylebone on June 20th and the following day between the Earls of Winchilsea and Darnley for 1,000 guineas'. So far as we have any knowledge, this is the only illustration to depict a game of cricket on Thomas Lord's original ground. Fortunately, however, it is not the only illustration to depict the first Lord's. Throughout the time that the infant MCC was starting to become established, the country at large was under great threat of invasion from Napoleon's France. A 'Dad's Army' fervour gripped the country. One result of this state of affairs was that the new cricket ground proved to be a popular place on which to stage military parades. The British Library is the possessor of two very fine watercolours by Henry Matthews. These depict the presentation of colours to the 2nd and 3rd Regiments of the Royal East India Volunteers at Lord's in 1797.

Print depicting the 'Grand Match' of 20 June 1793, as published in the *Sporting Magazine*.

Above: This watercolour by Henry Matthews shows the Consecration of Colours to the 3rd Regiment, Royal East India Volunteers, 1797.

Below: Also by Henry Matthews, this watercolour represents the Presentation of Colours to the 2nd Regiment, Royal East India Volunteers.

An even better contemporary impression of the original ground is to be seen in a painting which is housed in the Museum at the Bank of England. This very interesting work by Thomas Stothard shows Thomas Lord standing on a rostrum, which had been erected on his ground, and watching as the wives of the directors of the Bank presented colours. The recipients were members of the Bank of England Volunteers. It is believed that the Chief Cashier of the Bank exceeded his brief in commissioning this painting and, as a result, the artist had to wait a long time before he received any payment. If this be the case we should be very grateful that all turned out well in the end because it is our best evidence for the appearance of the original ground. The painting was commissioned in 1799 and at this time the place looked very rural. This state of affairs was not destined to last for much longer; London was expanding greatly and the resulting increase in the

rent, which was needed for the ground, was a crucial factor in eventually persuading Thomas Lord to transfer his precious turf to pastures new.

MCC has in its possession silhouettes of the founder and of his wife, Mr Walter Townsend having presented these artefacts to Lords in 1897. In addition the club has on display the famous portrait of Thomas which his descendant, Miss Florence Lord, gave in 1930. One of the most interesting physical links with the founder and the early days of the ground is a very beautiful punch bowl, which MCC was able to acquire in 1985. It was made in Jingdezhen in China and, according to the experts at the British Museum, may be dated to around the year 1786. On the outside of the bowl there is a willow-pattern type treatment given to the

Thomas Stothard's painting showing Lord's original ground. It depicts the presentation of colours to the Bank of England Volunteers at Lord's in 1799. (Bank of England Museum.)

A game of cricket taking place in 1790 (showing the recently introduced middle stump).

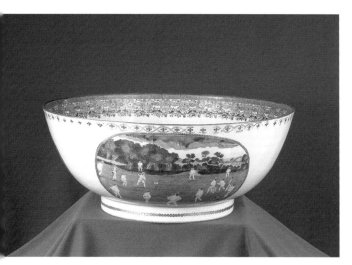

These two photographs show the punchbowl that may have been commissioned by Thomas Lord himself.

famous Hayman picture of cricket in the Marylebone Fields. On the inside there is to be seen a British vessel bearing the name 'Thirxs'. If this were intended to read Thirsk, it would seem to imply that this splendid piece was specially commissioned by none other than Thomas Lord himself and named after his native town. Whatever may be the truth of this, the scholars at the British Museum declare that, so far as they are aware, this is the only piece of Chinese export ceramics to depict cricket.

Another very interesting connection with the early days of Lord's is contained in the City of Westminster Archive Collection. This is a ticket for the MCC Anniversary Dinner, which was due to be held at 5.30 p.m. on Saturday 26 April 1800. This ticket may perhaps serve as a reminder that MCC is not only a very long-established cricketing institution, but it is also one of the oldest London clubs. Only White's (established in 1693), Boodles (1762), Brookes (1764) and the Royal Thames Yacht Club (1775) are older.

So it came about that Lord's took over from Hambledon the role of the leading cricket ground of the day. A striking confirmation of this can be found in the realisation that in 1788 (which was only one year after the foundation of the club) MCC took upon itself the mantle

of Hambledon and assumed responsibility for the revision of the laws of cricket.

A remarkable visual reminder of the link between the two great early centres of the game is to be found in a watercolour sketch executed by George Shepheard in around 1790. This not only shows Thomas Lord with the early stalwarts of Hambledon – such as David Harris, 'Old Everlasting' Walker and 'Silver Billy' Beldham – but also depicts some of the aristocratic members of the infant MCC – such as Captain Bligh, Colonel Tufton and Lord Frederick Beauclerk. We shall hear more about that fascinating character, Lord Frederick Beauclerk, in due course. It is also worth noting that in recent times MCC has been able to purchase a further sketch by Shepheard, showing another representation of Colonel Tufton.

Thomas Lord was always a good businessman and he accordingly realised that cricket is always liable to be rather a financial risk. This is, of course, particularly the case when the summer weather is unseasonable. One of Lord's more enterprising ploys was to stage a balloon ascent from the ground on 5 July 1802. This seems in all probability to have been made possible as a by-product of the Peace of Amiens, as it was an Anglo-French enterprise conducted by Mr Garnerin and Mr E.H. Locker: it is to be hoped that these gentlemen resisted the temptation to discuss the contemporary political scene!

There is no doubting, however, that cricket was the main *raison d'être* of the ground. It was in the historic year of 1805 (shortly before the Battle of Trafalgar) that there took place at Lord's the first in the long series of matches between Eton and Harrow. This is the oldest contest in the Lord's fixture list and the only one which is currently played to have been started on the original ground. Batsman number nine for Harrow on this occasion was none other than the famous poet, Lord Byron. One cannot help wondering whether, in view of his club foot, he needed a runner.

*T*HE Honour of your Company is defired at the Annniverfary Dinner of the CRICKET CLUB at LORD's Cricket-Ground, Mary-le-bone, on SATURDAY, the 26th of April, 1800, at Half paft Five o'Clock.

An Anfwer is defired, that Dinner may be provided accordingly.

N. B. Several Gentlemen intend Playing in the Morning.

CRAFT, Printer, Wells-ftreet, Oxford-ftreet.

Ticket for the MCC Anniversary Dinner of 1800.
(City of Westminster Archive Service.)

Sketch by George Shepheard showing Hambledon and MCC members, including Thomas Lord, 1790.

The laws of cricket, as revised by the MCC in 1788.

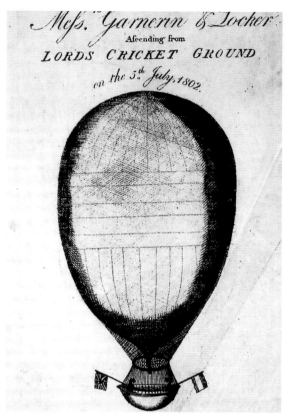

Bill poster showing one of the more adventurous attempts to generate revenue by Thomas Lord.

In a letter which has been preserved in the archives of Harrow School, the poet wrote: 'We have played the Eton and were most confoundedly beat, however it was some comfort to me that I got 11 notches the 1st innings and 7 the 2nd.' This letter may have been inspired more by poetic licence than by any great desire for factual accuracy. The scorebook of the match, which is nowadays in the possession of Eton College, does not seem to support the version of events which Lord Byron gave. This book is perhaps the oldest of its kind in existence. It was lost for a period of about 100 years and it looks in rather a mess. This is not surprising in view of the fact that it was used for some time by a farmer as his account book!

The following year, 1806, saw the first in the long and distinguished series of matches between Gentlemen and Players, which lasted until 1962. The decision in the following off-season to abolish amateur status in the first-class game inevitably had the sad consequence that this great and historic fixture would have to come to an end.

Perhaps the most vivid account of the first Lord's is contained in a book that bears the somewhat unpromising title of *Ius Ecclesiasticum Anglicanum*. The sub-title is rather more informative if only slightly more inviting: 'The laws of the Church of England Exemplified and Illustrated.' This unlikely source of very valuable information on the first Lord's Cricket Ground was published in 1810.

The author of this volume was a certain Dr Nathaniel Highmore, who reveals himself in his writings to have been a very embittered cleric. His main grievance seems to have been centred around his allegation that he had been prevented by the Archbishop of Canterbury from acting as a stipendiary clergyman whilst he was simultaneously engaged as an advocate in the ecclesiastical courts. The factor which proved to have been particularly annoying to the querulous Dr Highmore was the realisation that Lord Frederick Beauclerk was allowed to play cricket during most days in the summer although he held a cure of souls as Vicar of St Albans. Dr Highmore thought, with probably some justification, that the fact that Lord Frederick was the son of a duke might have had some bearing on the matter.

The trouble seems to have commenced in June 1808 when Highmore saw an advertisement in the *Morning Herald* which read: 'CRICKET – Grand match will be played in Lord's Cricket Ground, St Mary-le-bone on Thursday next June 23rd and the following day between the Gentlemen of the Homerton Club with T. Melluish Esq., Lambert, Hammond and T. Walker against eight of the county of Essex with Lord F. Beauclerk, B. Aislabie, G. Burrell Esq., Beldam (sic) and – Pontifex Esq for 1,000 guineas a side. The wickets to be pitched at 11 o'clock…Admittance sixpence. NO DOGS ADMITTED.'

Seldom can the Primate of All England have been submitted to such a stream of correspondence about the cricketing antics of one of his clergy – Dr Highmore duly wrote to the Archbishop to say that he was curious to see how Lord Frederick 'might violate with impunity the Church's law, by advertising himself for a public cricket player and gambler, to be seen as such by any man who would pay his sixpence'. The disgruntled cleric went especially to Lord's on the day advertised for the match. He later wrote 'After walking some little time about the spacious area destined for this very curious clerical exhibition, I went up to the booth. When I had stood there, on the outside (for the entrance seemed to belong only to the initiated and privileged) during a short time, I noticed a man coming out of the booth, dressed in a white hat, coloured handkerchief around his neck, striped trousers and a square kind of

coat…' Highmore thereupon enquired as to who this man might be. In reply his neighbour said that it was Lord Frederick Beauclerk. Highmore in response mentioned that he thought Lord Frederick was in holy orders. 'A clergyman' replied the neighbour, 'Why, so he is, but he ne'er preaches once of a twelvemonth!' Spurred on by this experience, the indefatigable Dr Highmore tried in vain to persuade the Archbishop of Canterbury to prevent Lord Frederick from playing cricket.

Further advertisements continued to appear in the *Morning Herald* throughout the duration of the 1808 season. These caused Dr Highmore to make the comment that no attempt had apparently been made by the leaders

The Revd Lord Frederick Beauclerk was President of MCC in 1826. This portrait is attributed to Sir William Beechey and was presented anonymously to MCC in 1993.

Rural Sports or a Cricket Match Extra Ordinary
by Thomas Rowlandson, 1811.

of the church to stop 'so shameful a violation of public decency'. Dr Highmore was to continue his campaign into the following year. On 15 July 1809 he sent to the long-suffering authorities at Lambeth Palace a cutting from the *British Press*, which announced that copies could be obtained from Mr Lord of the revised laws of cricket. Dr Highmore could not resist making the sly dig that there had been no revision of the laws of the Church of England.

Dr Highmore may well have been an embittered bore, but he did certainly highlight a danger in the early game – namely the excessive amount of gambling which was a pronounced feature of cricket at the start of the nineteenth century. He also vividly described the colourful

dress that was in vogue at the time. The colours which were used by the club at this date were sky blue. It is not certain that the famous 'egg and bacon' (or 'rhubarb and custard') came into being before the decade of the 1860s. This latter period was also the time when the club's celebrated monogram would first appear to have come into general use.

An event happened in 1992, which would have caused Dr Highmore to turn in his grave. In that year a very generous anonymous benefactor presented to MCC the striking portrait of Lord Frederick which has from time to time been attributed to Sir William Beechey. Lord Frederick became President of MCC in 1826 and he is thus the second person we know to have held this high office.

Among the early Lord's worthies one must mention Beauclerk's protégé, 'Squire' George Osbaldeston, and E.H. Budd. Osbaldeston is the first cricketer of note to have been educated at that great nursery of the game, Brasenose College, Oxford. He played his first match on the original Lord's in 1808. He later gave up his seat in Parliament because 'it was not exactly in accordance with his taste'. He was a great all-round sportsman even if it was somewhat of an exaggeration to say, as some were wont to do, that he was the greatest hunter since the days of the Assyrian Nimrod!

E.H. Budd was a very hard hitter of the ball. Indeed, on one occasion he despatched the ball clean out of the original Lord's. The bat with which this feat was accomplished is still on public display at the headquarters of cricket. Lord had offered a prize of £20 for such a feat. Budd proposed to distribute this sum among the players but, sad to relate, Thomas Lord does not seem to have honoured his word. Budd had a very long and distinguished career. He made his debut on the original ground, whilst his swansong for MCC was to be in the match against the recently founded Marlborough College fifty years later.

A map showing the locations of the grounds MCC has occupied. These include the Dorset Square site (1787-1811), the North Bank Area (1811-1814) and the present Lord's.

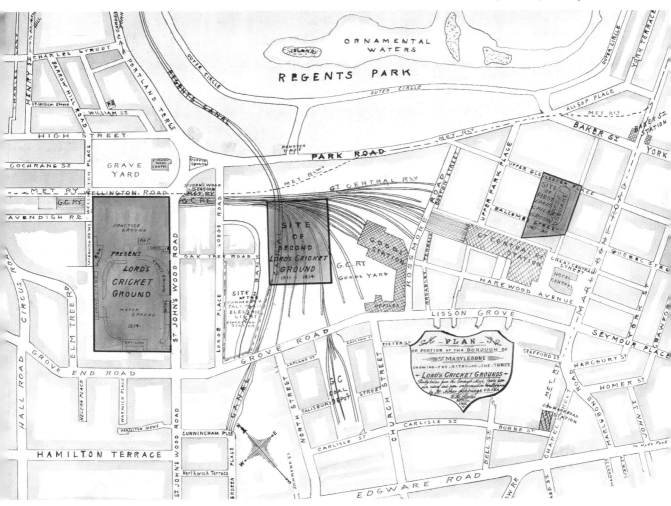

A portrait of William Beldham by A. Vincent, *c.* 1860.

Three great professionals also adorned the first Lord's. Tom Walker was a Hambledon veteran whose dogged defence was to earn for him the nickname of 'Old Everlasting'. He made the first recorded century to have been scored on the ground – 107 for MCC *v.* Middlesex in 1792. Four other hundreds were to follow from his bat when he played at Lord's.

'Silver Billy' Beldham was another veteran from the days of Hambledon. Indeed, he was the only one of these immortal heroes to have survived long enough to have been able to witness the age of photography. Silver Billy indeed lived every one of his ninety-six years to the full. He made a score of 144 in the same match in which Tom Walker amassed his historic century. He also scored two hundreds when he played for Surrey on the original ground. There is preserved in the collection at Lord's a clock whose case was made from timbers which had been taken from Beldham's cottage near Farnham in Surrey. One can also see on display at Lord's a portrait of Silver Billy.

William Lambert belonged to a slightly later generation. He was a highly competent all-rounder who made two centuries on the original Lord's. His greatest feat, however, belonged to a later period. He made the first recorded feat of scoring a century in each innings of an important match. This was on the occasion when he made 107 not out and 157 at Lord's in 1817 whilst he appeared for Sussex against Epsom. It is indeed very sad to have to report that he did not play again at the headquarters of cricket after that season. He was alleged to have 'sold' the England *v.* Nottingham match (although Sir Pelham Warner in his well-known book on Lord's is characteristically inclined to give Lambert the benefit of the doubt).

One other event of considerable importance happened when the original Lord's was in operation. In 1800 Thomas Boxall broke new ground with his *Rules and Instructions for Playing at the Game of Cricket*. This was dedicated to MCC. In his inscription to the members of MCC, the rather fulsome Mr Boxall wrote:

'My Lords and Gentlemen –

Duly impressed with frequent repetition of your goodness, I have, with the utmost deference, presumed to offer this small, but I flatter myself useful, tract of the utmost important article of performing that useful and noble game of cricket. Conscious of your kindness, I thus fearless approach you, being fully convinced that, however trifling the subject, when due exertions have been attempted, you will not cast, hurtfully to the performer, the futile attempt, under such impressions, my Lords and Gentlemen, I have devoted a portion of my time in penning these articles which may guide the inexperienced to the full attainment of the knowledge which may be conducive to their satisfaction, while it advances their health, which, that you may ever enjoy, is the earnest wish of, my Lords and Gentlemen.
Your devoted and obedient servant.
T. Boxall.'

After one has made all due allowances for Mr Boxall's rather florid style, one can note two important facts. First, this book was the earliest instructional volume in the history of the game and, secondly, it is clear that by the dawn of the nineteenth century, the youthful MCC was a very significant club and *the* force to be reckoned with in the world of cricket.

Another indication of the importance of MCC around this time is afforded in the account which was given in the *Life and Times of Frederick Reynolds*. The author of this autobiography wrote:

'The day I was proposed as a member of the Marylebone Club, then in its highest fashion, I waited at the Portland Coffee House to hear from Tom Lord the result of the ballot with more anxiety than I experienced the month before, while expecting the decision of the audience on my play. Being unanimously elected, I immediately assumed the sky-blue dress, the uniform of the club and soon thoroughly entered into all the spirit of this new and gay scene.'

London was experiencing considerable expansion at this time. The rent for the ground was rising fast, but Thomas Lord had had the very considerable foresight to hire on 15 October 1800 the Brick Field and the Great Field at North Bank. This area was situated on the Eyre Estate in the then very rural St John's Wood. This was for a term of eighty years free of land tax and tithe at £54 per annum. The ground was all ready in 1809, but it was not until another two years had elapsed that the new Lord's was taken over officially. This took place on 8 May 1811. The sacred turf was removed from the Dorset Fields ground so that the 'noblemen and gentlemen of the MCC should be able to play on the same footing as before'.

The new ground did not prove to be very popular, however, and not all that many matches were played on it.

A solution to this dilemma came from a most unexpected source. Parliament decreed that the new Regent's Canal should be cut through the centre of the ground. A further move was thus imperative. Once again the members of the Eyre family came to the rescue. The Eyre Estate provided a new plot slightly further to the north of the old ground and the turf was transferred in time for the start of the 1814 season. It was fortunate that MCC made this move – quite apart from the digging of the canal, the building of the St John's Wood Power Station and the coming of the railways later on would probably have made the club's retention of the second ground untenable. As it was, with the move to the third Lord's, the nomadic existence of the MCC was thankfully at an end.

two

1814 – 1837
CONSOLIDATION

This splendid portrait of Benjamin Aislabie was painted by
W. Novice in 1814.

The third Lord's Cricket Ground opened very dramatically – not with a whimper but with a bang. There was a very large explosion at the 'new' Lord's cricket ground public house, Marylebone Fields, four days before the venue was due to be opened. Quite what was the reason for the landlady finding it necessary to have considerable quantities of gunpowder in her possession does not seem ever to have become very clear.

The first official function to be held on the new ground was, one would hope, a somewhat quieter affair. A reception was laid on for the Bishop of London, who had just consecrated the adjacent St John's Wood Church. Mrs Lord was in due course to be laid to rest in the adjoining burial ground. There she has for company J.S. Cotman of the Norwich School of painters and Joanna Southcott, the religious fanatic and owner of the famous box.

Lord put in a self-explanatory advertisement in the *Morning Post* for 7 May 1814: 'T. Lord respectfully informs the Noblemen, Gentlemen, Members of the Marylebone and St John's Wood Cricket Club, that the new ground is completely ready for playing on and that the first meeting of the Marylebone Club will be on Monday 9th May and continue every Monday, Wednesday and Friday during the season. The New Road leading to it is commodiously finished, the entrance which is opposite Marylebone Workhouse or up Baker Street North, which is upwards of half a mile nearer than the old road up Lisson Grove.'

The first match on the ground of which we have any record took place on 22 June 1814. On this very memorable occasion MCC were victorious over Hertfordshire by the comfortable margin of an innings and 27 runs. 'Squire' George Osbaldeston, Lord Frederick Beauclerk, E.H. Budd and William Ward all played their part in the match. These were numbered among the most prominent amateurs of the day. William Ward, in particular, was destined to play an ever more important role in the affairs of MCC as the days went by.

With this latest move, MCC had at long last acquired a permanent home. Lord's now very obviously needed a competent secretary to oversee its affairs. Cometh the hour cometh the man – in 1822 such a person was fortunately readily forthcoming in the shape (soon to be the very substantial shape) of Benjamin Aislabie. Like Thomas Lord himself, this cricketer was a wine merchant by profession. He also has the distinction of being alluded to in *Tom Brown's Schooldays*, being depicted in this classic book as taking a cricket team to play for MCC at Rugby School. Aislabie's snuffbox is still to be seen – it is on display in the MCC Museum.

It is perhaps instructive to compare two paintings of him, which are housed at cricket's headquarters. There is a very attractive portrait by W. Novice, showing a slim and athletic-looking Aislabie on horseback. This painting was a great favourite of the late E.W. Swanton, the well-known

Benjamin Aislabie, Secretary of MCC, depicted in later life by H.E. Dawe.

A picture of William Ward, shown alongside the ball with which he scored 278 for MCC *v.* Norfolk in 1820. This remained a record at Lord's until 1925. Incidentally, this is the earliest surviving cricket ball and is pictured on top of his account book.

A letter dated 6 May 1834 from J.C. Ryle, the Eton captain, challenging his Harrow counterpart to a match at Lord's.

cricket writer. A subsequent portrait of Benjamin Aislabie depicts an overweight secretary who would certainly appear to have dined too well and perhaps unwisely. In 1914 the then Treasurer of MCC, Sir Spencer Ponsonby-Fane, reminisced that as a lad he saw 'Mr Benjamin Aislabie, the Secretary of the Club, a big fat man over twenty stone in weight, fussing about with a red book in which he was entering subscriptions for some desired match, of which the funds of the club could not afford the expenditure'.

In addition to witnessing the arrival at Lord's of Benjamin Aislabie, the year 1822 was in other important ways very significant in the annals of MCC. On 16 July of that year John Willes opened the bowling at Lord's for Kent in their match against MCC. For this, Willes used his customary round-arm delivery. At this date only under-arm deliveries were legal. The umpire promptly no-balled him. Willes was not the sort of man who would tolerate any opposition and he threw down the ball in disgust. He thereupon mounted his horse and, to quote H.S. Altham, one of the greatest of all historians of the game, 'he rode out of Lord's and first-class cricket for ever'.

Willes was not, however, alone in bowling round-arm. Two bowlers down in Sussex had also adopted his particular style of delivery. They were William Lillywhite and Jem Broadbridge. The authorities of MCC regarded their action as being in the category of throwing, but the Sussex supporters of the dissident pair called it rather grandiloquently 'the march of the intellect system'. Mr H.R. Kingscote, the MCC President in 1827, arranged that year for Sussex to challenge All-England in the best of three matches. In the first game at Sheffield, Sussex won by a margin of 7 wickets. Back at the headquarters of cricket that county was again victorious but on home ground down at Brighton they lost to England. The result was, however, only obtained (it was alleged) because one of the players adopted the 'intellect system'. He was a certain G.T. Knight, the nephew of Jane Austen.

Controversy raged in the pages of the *Sporting Magazine*, but in the end MCC belatedly bowed to the inevitable and in 1835 the club accepted round-arm bowling up as far as the shoulder instead of the elbow. Rule 10 still, however, was to insist that 'the ball must be bowled'. If it were thrown or jerked or if the hand were above the shoulder in the delivery, the umpire should have no option but to call a no ball.

In the meantime there were other incidents at Lord's which were, in their own way, just about as dramatic. The founder had shocked the entire cricketing establishment by boldly stating that he had received permission from the Eyre Estate to develop part of the outfield for a housing project. The result of this proposal, if it had gone through, would have been that only 150 square yards would have been left for the playing area. It was another instance of cometh the hour, cometh the man. Thomas Lord's plans horrified those who were in the know. None was more put out by the news than William Ward. He wrote out a cheque for £5,000 and, in so doing, saved the ground for our national game. Ward was a member of a well-known family from the Isle of Wight. In addition he had a very busy public life, serving as a Director of the Bank of England and as the Member of Parliament for the City of London. MCC has recently been able to acquire William Ward's account book. This gives fascinating details into many esoteric corners connected with the history of

cricket. From it one can learn, for example, the cost of cricket bats at the time and the amount of money which was expended in purchasing water troughs for the sheep. This is a reminder that Lord's was a very rural ground in atmosphere in those days.

Ward was a very imposing person – he was a large and powerfully built man, standing over six feet in height and weighing in the region of 14 stone. He was to be the proprietor of Lord's for a period of ten years from 1825 until 1835. Back in 1820, he had amassed a score of 278 when he played for MCC in the match against Norfolk. This innings was to remain a record for the ground until it was surpassed 105 years later in 1925. One can still see in the

A silhouette of the controversial bowler, John Willes.

MR. JOHN WILLES

MCC Museum the ball off which Ward scored these runs. Indeed, it is reliably believed to be the oldest cricket ball to have survived anywhere.

Ward's family were to become prominent members of the high church Oxford Movement. It is therefore appropriate that in 1825 (the year in which Ward took over the ground) the future Cardinal Manning turned out for the Harrow XI. In the MCC Library there is preserved a letter which Manning wrote in his old age in which he refers nostalgically to this match.

Ward had almost literally a baptism of fire when he took over at Lord's. In the early hours of 29 July 1825 the pavilion burned to the ground. *The Times* was to report the next day: 'From the nature of the materials, which were chiefly of wood, albeit enlarged and beautified at a great expense, the fire in a very short time defied the power of the fire engines and water, if there had been a sufficient supply which happened not to be the case. In about an hour and a half after the commencement of the fire, the whole pavilion was reduced to a heap of ruins, saving only the foundation.' *John Bull* for Sunday 31 July further catalogued the tale of woe: 'There was in the pavilion a large and valuable stock of wine, the property of the subscribers, which along with all their cricketing apparatus, no longer exists.' *The Morning Post* for 30 July 1825 was not above some mischief making: 'It is a curious fact that a grand match was to have been played yesterday in the ground, between the scholars of Harrow School and Eton College, and that some of the parties enjoyed themselves in the early part of Thursday.'

The show had to go on, however. On the very next morning the advertised match took place but, sad to relate, all of the club's early records went up in smoke in the course of that fateful night of ill omen.

One famous series of matches saw its origin at this time. Charles Wordsworth of Christ Church instituted the Varsity match between Oxford and Cambridge. He was a nephew of William Wordsworth, the celebrated poet, and in addition he was the son of the Master of Trinity

College, Cambridge. Charles also had a brother who was being educated at the latter university and he thus had a foot in both educational camps, so to speak. It is quite evident that he was a paragon of all the nineteenth-century virtues. In addition to his pioneering work for cricket, he was also instrumental in founding the Boat Race in 1829. In the fullness of time, and perhaps inevitably, he became a bishop. He was, however, refreshingly human. Writing over sixty years later, the aged Bishop Wordsworth had this to say when describing his need to obtain permission to leave Oxford in term time to play at Lord's: 'My conscience still rather smites me when I remember that in order to gain my end, I had to present myself to the Dean and tell him that I wished to go to London – not to play a game of cricket (that would not have been listened to) but to consult a dentist… at all events, my tutor, Longley – afterwards Archbishop of Canterbury – was privy to it'.

The present writer is pleased to think that his mother, as a little girl, met Charles's nephew – John Wordsworth, the then Bishop of Salisbury. It is good to have this slight link with the early days in the history of Lord's. The oldest scorebook to be preserved in the Library at Lord's includes details of the 1829 Varsity match, which was held in Oxford on the Magdalen College Ground.

In 1830 Sir George Everest (after whom the highest mountain in the world is named) used Lord's to test methods of measuring long distances. He had the assistance of cadets from the Royal Military Academy, Woolwich. He paid MCC £24 for the hire of Lord's for three weeks.

A great link with the past was severed in 1832 with the death of Thomas Lord, the founder. He had gone into retirement to the little Hampshire village of West Meon and was buried in the churchyard there. MCC, as is only right and proper, has taken on itself some responsibility for the upkeep of the grave. This was renovated in 1951 by the long-established Winchester firm of monumental masons, Messrs Vokes and Beck. A small part of the original tombstone is now incorporated into the memorial to the well-known cricket historian, H.S. Altham, in the

A print of Charles Wordsworth.

The jubilee match was played at Lord's between North and South in 1837.

MCC Museum. In the club's bicentenary year of 1987, the first function to take place happened on 13 January (the 155th anniversary of Lord's death) when Colin Cowdrey (the then President of MCC) laid a wreath on the grave in the midst of a raging blizzard.

The earliest membership list for MCC dates from the year 1822, when 202 members were recorded as being on the club's books. Eight professional bowlers were engaged during the period of the cricket season and six boys were employed as scouts. Practice days were Tuesdays, Wednesdays and Saturdays during the months of May, June and July. The annual dinner took place at the Clarendon Hotel and cost the princely sum of three guineas. At the start of 1835, the club's membership comprised of one Duke, two Marquises, eleven Earls, eight Baronets, twenty-three Honourables and nearly 200 other gentlemen.

MCC has preserved in its keeping a letter which was written by J.C. Ryle, the Captain of the Eton XI in 1834. In it he challenged his counterpart at Harrow to a match. It is pleasing to note that Ryle became in due course the first Bishop of Liverpool. This is the see which has recently been vacated by another cricketer, Lord Sheppard.

In 1835 William Ward transferred the lease of Lord's, with fifty-eight years left, to Mr J.H. Dark for £2,000 and an annuity of £425. The Dark family were to remain intimately connected with the headquarters of cricket for a period of over 100 years. Dark was the son of a saddler and was born in the Edgware Road on 24 May 1795. He started his working life on the Dorset Fields ground and he was to be connected with Lord's all his life. Only the Gaby family can rival the Darks in terms of length of service to the ground.

1837 saw the accession to the throne of the young Queen Victoria. A fresh start seemed to be offered thereby to the nation and the year was also notable in the annals of Lord's. At that time MCC celebrated its Golden Jubilee. Benjamin Aislabie entered the following in the minute book on 30 July 1836: 'The Marylebone Club having been established in the year 1787, it is resolved that a Jubilee

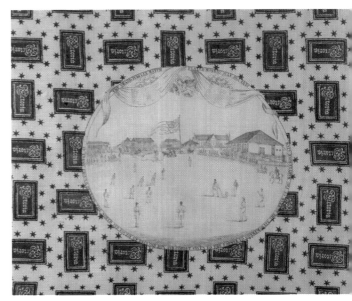

Cloth showing the jubilee match of 1837.

Goblet made to celebrate the jubilee of MCC in 1837.

Match shall take place at Lord's Ground on the second Monday in July 1837, for the benefit of the players, twenty-two of whom shall be chosen to perform on that day. The Earl of Thanet and the Lord Frederick Beauclerk are requested to make the selection and every member of the club is solicited for a subscription of one pound towards the promotion of the sport on this interesting occasion.'

In the event, the match took place in a slightly subdued mood just two days after the funeral of King William IV. MCC has in its possession prints of this match. Round the edge of one of these can be seen masses of patriotic symbols proclaiming the accession of the young Queen Victoria. A goblet, which was made to commemorate the Jubilee Match, also survives and is on display at Lord's.

With the advent of J.H. Dark and with the celebration of MCC's first jubilee, a new era had arrived at Lord's.

three

1837 – 1866
EARLY VICTORIANS

J.H. Dark as drawn by John Corbet Anderson in 1852.

J.H. Dark came in like a lion and, like the month of March, went out of Lord's like a lamb. To celebrate the club's golden jubilee in an appropriate manner, a grand dinner was held after the special match – in which the South was victorious over the North. The banquet was 'served up in Mr Dark's usual excellent style and consisted of every delicacy of the season'.

It must have been round about this time that the great Sir Spencer Ponsonby-Fane first visited Lord's. Writing in 1914 and recording some of his memories of about eighty years before, he reminisced:

'Whilst I was still a lad, Mr Dark, then proprietor of the ground and who paid all expenses connected with it, presented me with a bat and the "Freedom of the Ground" as he called it. From that time I was there continually, and I may almost say have lived there up to the present day. Oh what changes I have seen and taken part in, not only in the scene itself but the nature and exponents of the game. It is only natural that in such a length of time such changes should have taken place, but it is almost impossible to compare the rough and simple habits of those times with the luxury of the present day.

'In the pavilion, a small-roomed building, surrounded with a few laurels and shrubs and capable of holding forty or fifty members, I can see Mr Benjamin Aislabie, the Secretary of the Club… and here sat Lord Frederick Beauclerk, then the autocrat of the club and of cricket in general, laying down the law and organising the game. On these he always had a bet of a sovereign and he himself managed them whilst sitting alongside the scorers at the top of the ground, when he issued his orders to the players, he himself had then given up playing.

'Then there was the public house, a long low building on the south side, separated from the ground by a row of clipped lime trees and a few green benches on which the thirsty spectators smoked long pipes and enjoyed drinks. Round the ground there were more of these small benches without backs, and a pot-boy walked round with a supply of beer, a porter for the public who had no other means of refreshing themselves. Excepting these benches, there were no seats for spectators. At the south-east corner of the ground there were large stacks of willow blocks to be seasoned and made into bats in the workshop adjoining. On the upper north-east corner was a large sheep pen. In the centre of the ground opposite the Pavilion was a square patch of grass, which was kept constantly rolled and taken care of. No scythe was allowed to touch it and mowing machines were not then invented.

'The rest of the ground was ridge and furrow – not very easy for playing on, nor made any easier by the number of old pitches which abounded, for on non-match days the public could have a pitch for a shilling, a sum which included the use of stumps, bat and ball, the first-named selected from half a dozen or so from the capacious breeches of "Steevie" Slatter, Mr Dark's factotum, which never seemed to be empty.

'The grass as I have said was never mowed. It was usually kept down by a flock of sheep which were penned up on match days and on Saturdays four or five hundred were on to the ground on their way to the Monday Smithfield Market. It was marvellous to see how they cleared the

A view of Lord's from around 1837. The sheep are clearly visible as is the Roman Catholic church in Lisson Grove, which was built in 1836.

A painting of John Wisden, by William Bromley (1835-1888).

herbage. From the pitch itself, selected by Mr Dark, half a
dozen boys picked on the rough stalks of the grass. The
wickets were sometimes difficult – in a dry north-west
wind for instance – but when they were in good order it
was a joy to play on them, they were so full of life and
spirit. The creases were cut with a knife and, though more
destructive to the ground, were more accurate than those
marked subsequently with white paint.'

Sir Spencer went on to say: 'The ordinary dress of the
day included a flannel jacket of short cut and a tall hat and
I can say that the latter was no more uncomfortable than
the billycock which succeeded it as headwear. Wisden was
the first professional who wore a straw hat before the

introduction of the cricket cap. There was no such thing
as pads or finger guards in those days.

They didn't mind a few stingers
And they didn't wear India-rubber fingers.

When leg pads were first introduced they were worn
under the trousers, as though a hardy cricketer was
ashamed of his cowardice in wearing them.'

In 1838 (the year following the jubilee of MCC) two
disparate events took place at Lord's. On a rather mundane
but practical note the pavilion was lit by gas for the first
time. Perhaps more significantly, in the same year,
J.H. Dark opened a court for real tennis. In William
Denison's book *Matches of the Players* we read:

A print of the old real tennis courts at Lord's.

Real tennis rackets from a seventeenth-century carving, believed to be from Hatfield House.

'In 1838 he (Dark) erected a capacious tennis court at an expense of upwards of £4,000, a proceeding which has tended very considerably to increase the membership of the Mary-le-bone Club, seeing that more than 150, amongst whom are the finest nobles of the land, have enrolled their name since the completion of the building.'

The fees that were charged seem to have been on the low side: 1s set for members and 1s 6d for strangers, all fees to be paid by the losers. Gentlemen playing with markers could charge 1s for a 'love set'. In this way Lord's became a leading centre for real tennis, which is a game of even greater antiquity than cricket (indeed, the sport can claim the distinction of being mentioned in Shakespeare). In due

course, as we shall see, this led to a very formative and influential role for the MCC in the development of lawn tennis in the early stages of that game. In addition, real tennis is to be seen in the oldest item that is in the possession of MCC: a sixteenth-century Flemish panel painting showing the Old Testament story of David and Bathsheba.

In 1840 the first match was played between MCC and Rugby School at Lord's. The famous game, which is immortalised in *Tom Brown's Schooldays*, actually took place at Rugby in the following year. 100 years on, in spite of the prevailing difficult wartime conditions, a great centenary match was held against Rugby School in 1941.

Back at Lord's, the ground was still in a rather primitive state. A description of the place written in 1841 states that the ground had a 'cottage-like pavilion with a few shrubs in front of it. Sandwiches and beer were the only refreshments except an ordinary tavern that gentlemen never went to. There was a miniature hill and valley between the farthest corner of the pavilion and the lower wicket and Lord's was more like a field pure and simple, but the rigour of the game was insisted on, and that was the ground to test a man's batting ability.'

With regard to the administration of the ground, that too seems to have been in rather a rudimentary state. In the year 1841, to take one example, the Hon. Frederick Ponsonby (the brother of Sir Spencer) announced that he proposed to raise a subscription in order that the Gentlemen *v.* Players match could be played. The MCC Committee did not apparently think that the game would be of sufficient interest to the general public as to warrant their support! Ponsonby's fine initiative, along with J.H. Dark's very generous underwriting of the 1842 match, enabled a celebrated Lord's fixture to become established.

Dark was at heart an entrepreneur. Perhaps his most bizarre achievement took place in August 1844. Dark arranged 'Under Noble and Distinguished Patronage Encampment of the Iowan Indians at Lord's Cricket Ground, St John's Wood for one week only. First time in Europe. Indian Archery Fete and Festival'. Among the

The oldest item in the possession of MCC, a sixteenth-century Flemish
panel painting, depicts a game of real tennis taking place.

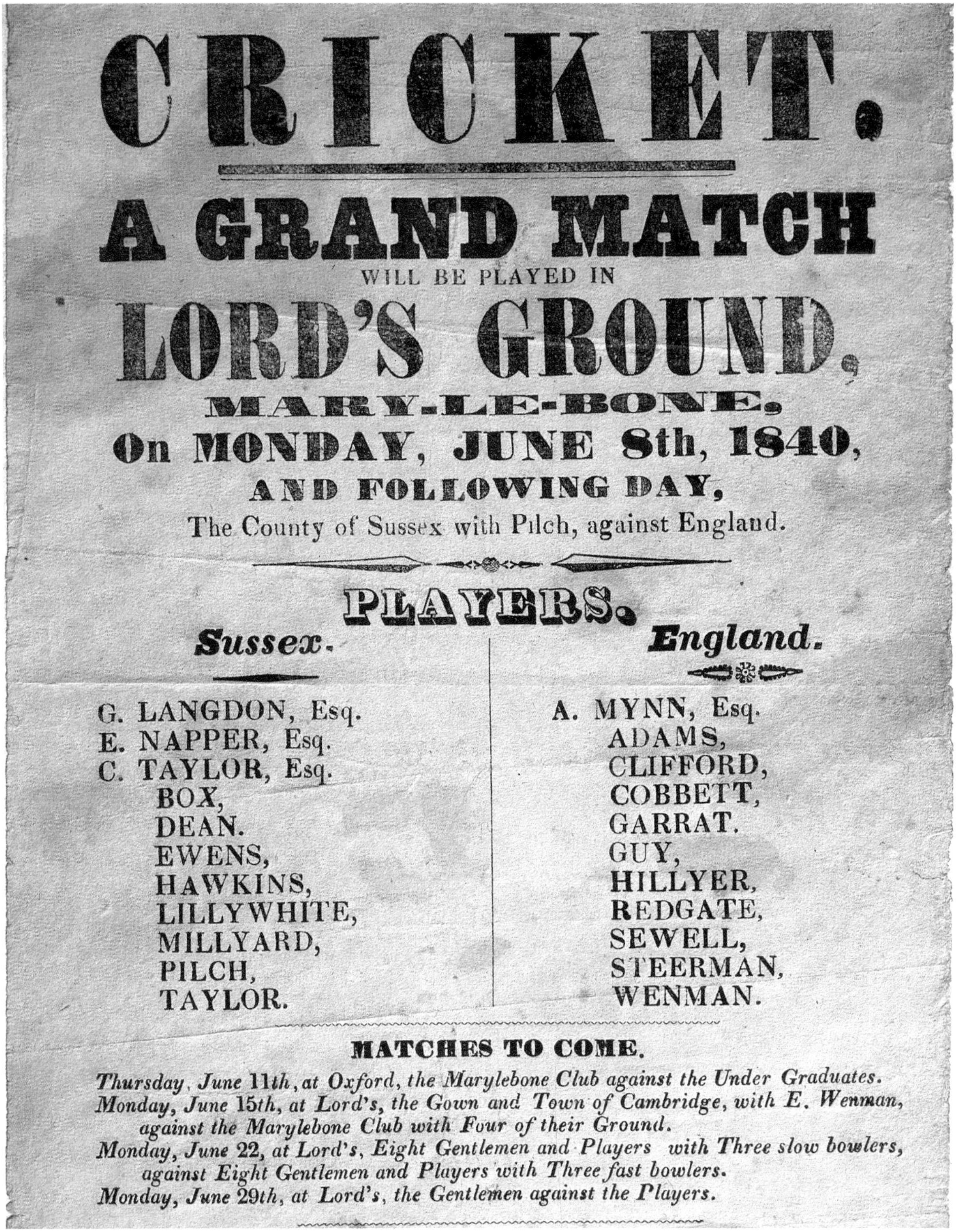

CRICKET.

A GRAND MATCH

WILL BE PLAYED IN

LORD'S GROUND,

MARY-LE-BONE.

On MONDAY, JUNE 8th, 1840,

AND FOLLOWING DAY,

The County of Sussex with Pilch, against England.

PLAYERS.

Sussex.	*England.*
G. LANGDON, Esq.	A. MYNN, Esq.
E. NAPPER, Esq.	ADAMS,
C. TAYLOR, Esq.	CLIFFORD,
BOX,	COBBETT,
DEAN.	GARRAT.
EWENS,	GUY,
HAWKINS,	HILLYER,
LILLYWHITE,	REDGATE,
MILLYARD,	SEWELL,
PILCH,	STEERMAN,
TAYLOR.	WENMAN.

MATCHES TO COME.

Thursday, June 11th, at Oxford, the Marylebone Club against the Under Graduates.
Monday, June 15th, at Lord's, the Gown and Town of Cambridge, with E. Wenman, against the Marylebone Club with Four of their Ground.
Monday, June 22, at Lord's, Eight Gentlemen and Players with Three slow bowlers, against Eight Gentlemen and Players with Three fast bowlers.
Monday, June 29th, at Lord's, the Gentlemen against the Players.

Bill poster advertising Sussex *v.* England at Lord's, 1840.

delegation was the splendidly named Mew-Hu-She-Kaw ('White Chief'), who was the first Chief of the Nation. We do not know whether or not Dark regarded this event as being a success, but it was never repeated.

Perhaps less controversially, 1846 saw the installation of the first telegraph scoreboard at Lord's. This showed runs, wickets down and the score of the last man out. Two years later, in 1848, a printing tent appeared. On 26 June that year the public could, for the very first time at Lord's, buy a card of the match. Frederick Lillywhite supervised the printing tent and it was a portable affair that was removed at the end of a major fixture.

As we have already seen, the first Varsity match was played at Lord's back in 1827, but it was only in 1851 (the year of the Great Exhibition) that this historic fixture was to find a regular home at the headquarters of cricket. In general, however, it must be admitted that the 1850s and the early part of the decade which followed were not to be numbered as being among Lord's finest hours. Edward Rutter wrote of the ground in his *Cricket Memories*:

'The reader will be surprised to hear that the matches there in the fifties and sixties were mostly of no interest except to the players themselves. Scratch teams of amateurs against the club with bowler and suchlike comprised most of them… Lord's was heavy clay and badly drained and the out-fielding was always rough and treacherous. There were no boundaries – except the pavilion – no stands or fixed seats of any kind, nothing but the small club pavilion and a line of loose benches running part of the way round the ground and these were but little occupied save at the most important matches.

'The ground in most matches therefore presented rather a dreary scene. To anyone but the committee as it was then constituted, it was becoming evident that the club was in danger of losing its influence.'

We have the authority of no less a person than Dr W.G. Grace himself, who wrote in his famous book, *Cricket*:

'The contests of the year were the All England XI *v.* The United XI, and the North *v.* South at Lord's.

Especially the former. When the two famous Elevens met, reputations were at stake, and both strove to put their best in the field… It was the match of the year… and crowds testified to it by turning out in the thousands. It was not always so in the North *v.* South matches.'

The All-England XI was a speculative venture, which had been founded by William Clark of Nottingham. If he had a fault it lay in the fact that he was a rather dictatorial character whose brusque manner upset some players. The

Below: Native Americans at Lord's in 1844.
Bottom: Athletics at Lord's in 1842.

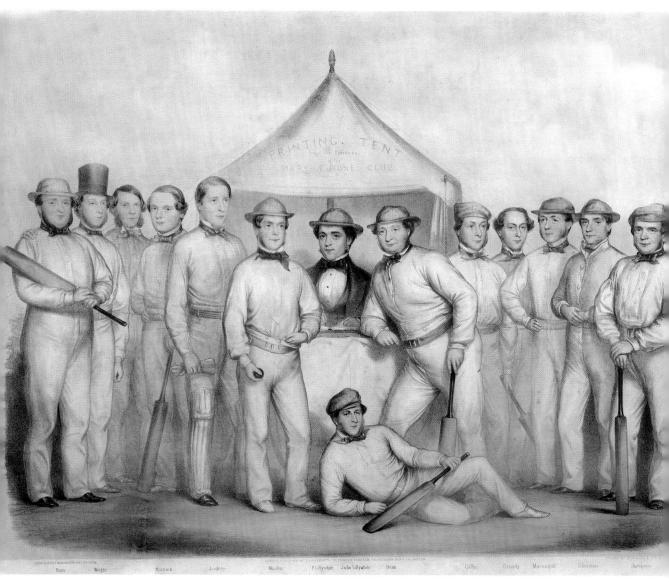

The United England XI in front of the printing tent.

rival United England XI was set up by those great cricketers James Dean and John Wisden. Clarke died in 1845
and in his place the more genial George Parr took over
the reins. The latter was soon afterwards to lead the first
overseas touring team, which had many adventures when
they travelled to and played in the United States and
Canada in 1859. George Parr was also the man who skip-
pered the second England tour of Australia in 1863/64.

It was a graphic illustration of the declining grip that
J.H. Dark had on the situation that in 1860 the freehold of
the ground was sold by the Eyre Estate but, almost unbe-
lievably, MCC did not even bother to put in a bid. The
purchaser was a certain Mr Moses. In spite of J.H. Dark's
increasing lassitude, however, he founded a family dynasty,
which had strong links with Lord's that lasted for over
100 years.

In 1863, this prevailing mood of inertia and lethargy was
abruptly to change with the inspired appointment of R.A.
Fitzgerald as Secretary of the MCC. He was not the sort of
person to let the grass grow under his feet – both literally
and metaphorically. He also altered his position from being
an honorary one to becoming a salaried occupation.

A watercolour from the sketchbook kept by Felix (Nicholas
Wanostrocht) showing Lord's in 1851.

Lord's cricket ground in 1851.

Portrait of George Parr by William Bromley.

Fitzgerald was in addition a keen photographer. In those more leisurely days he was able to tour the country and at weekends played much country house cricket, visiting amongst other people and places Althorp and the newly-built Sandringham (where he met Edward, the Prince of Wales, and his beautiful young Danish wife, Princess Alexandra). At the former place his host was the 'Red Earl' Spencer. The parents of Queen Mary, the Prince and Princess of Teck, watched the match. On these occasions, Fitzgerald filled his scrapbooks with many photographs that he took himself. These are now preserved in the MCC Library and they form a very fascinating social and sporting commentary on country house cricket in its mid-Victorian heyday. Mr T.G. Fitzgerald, the grandson of the former MCC Secretary, kindly presented them to MCC.

Fitzgerald was, according to Edward Rutter:

'Full of energy and enthusiastically keen on making Lord's the great centre of cricket, as it should be. But the committee were deplorably lethargic and out of date, and the zealous Secretary could obtain little support. One of his schemes for advancing this desirable end was to attempt to induce Middlesex to play their matches at Lord's, for he could easily perceive that unless he could find something to attract the crowd it would soon become deserted… But Middlesex in the meantime had found a suitable ground at Prince's and Fitzgerald's offer was politely declined.'

Mr Rutter would have known precisely what he was talking about, because he was a member of the MCC Committee at various dates between the years 1873 and 1903. He reminds us what a limited fixture list was available at the headquarters of cricket in those years. There were, needless to say, no Test matches at that time, and Lord's still had some years to go before it was to become the headquarters of the Middlesex County Cricket Club.

Fitzgerald soon made considerable progress, however, and in 1864 the first groundsman was appointed. His name was David Jordan and he was engaged at the rate of 25s a week. Two other very encouraging events also hap-

pened in 1864. The initial edition of *Wisden Cricketers' Almanack* appeared and a fifteen-year-old boy named W.G. Grace stole the headlines by making 100 and 56 not out when he played against the Gentlemen of Sussex at Brighton. The great cricketer was to make his debut at Lord's the following year.

R.A. Fitzgerald was a gifted and witty Irishman – he was also a hard-hitting batsman. In 1865 the Lord's pavilion was enlarged and the following year the freehold was once again up for sale. This time the price had escalated to £18,333 6s 8d. Fitzgerald was not, however, one to waver. He saw to it that MCC went very promptly into action and the ground was purchased with the aid of money that had been very generously advanced by Mr William Nicholson MP. This public-spirited benefactor of MCC was liberal in all but his politics, having deserted that party for the Conservatives. He was a member of the famous gin family.

One of the earliest objects to display the famous MCC monograph – a boundary flag from the 1860s.

William Lillywhite.

As to the great players of this period, we have already encountered William Lillywhite, the *nonpareil*. He was born in 1792 and he only stood at 5ft 4in in height. He was a very accurate slow bowler, who invariably bowled round the wicket. His first match for the Players at Lord's was in 1820 and he did not make his last appearance in this fixture until 1849. He had reached the ripe old age of fifty-two when he joined the ground staff at Lord's. When he died in 1854, the club took on itself the responsibility for

the erection of a handsome memorial to him in Highgate Cemetery, where he keeps Karl Marx company. Only his surname appears on the gravestone – he did not need any other identification, it seems. He was, after all *the* Lillywhite, although other members of his family were by no means negligible in cricket or in the business world.

One of the most interesting and attractive cricketers of this period was the great Felix. He was a man of Flemish descent, whose real name was Nicholas Wanostrocht. He became a schoolmaster and it may have been because of this that he wanted to preserve his privacy by adopting the pseudonym 'Felix'. Alternatively, it may have been for the very simple yet compelling reason that few people could spell or pronounce his unusual Flemish name. Felix became a member of William Clarke's All England XI. He once played in a match at Lord's that was watched by Albert, the Prince Consort. Despite his Germanic origin, Prince Albert was chosen to be Patron of MCC. The club's Annual Report for 1843 observed – 'the national and manly game of cricket cannot but rise still more in public estimation under such distinguished patronage'.

As part of its ongoing publishing programme, MCC reproduced in 2002 the fascinating sketchbooks which Felix compiled as he accompanied the All England XI up and down the country 150 years ago. Included in them is a delightful watercolour that Felix executed when he played at Lord's in 1851. He was a very competent artist as well a great stalwart of the Kent XI and of the Gentlemen. In a moving tribute, Lord Bessborough (the brother of Sir Spencer Ponsonby-Fane) said of Felix:

'He was an enthusiastic player of cricket without any jealousy of the play of others, though burning to distinguish himself, and he was one of the cleverest, most accomplished, kind-hearted and truest friends I ever had.'

The great companion of Felix in the Kent team and in the Gentlemen's Eleven was his stalwart friend and colleague, Alfred Mynn. The latter was indeed often given the nickname 'Alfred the Great', not only on account of his tremendous cricketing skills but also because of his great

The All England XI of 1847, painted by Felix.

A GRAND MATCH
WILL BE PLAYED IN
LORD'S GROUND,
MARYLEBONE,

On Monday, June 28th, 1847, & following Day.

Kent against England.

PLAYERS.

Kent.	England.
E. L. BAYLEY, Esq.	Sir F. BATHURST
E. BANKS, Esq.	A. M. HOARE, Esq.
N. FELIX, Esq.	R. T. KING, Esq.
A. MYNN, Esq.	O. C. PELL, Esq.
ADAMS	BOX
DORRINTON	CLARK
HILLYER	DEAN
MARTIN	GUY
MARTINGEL	LILLYWHITE
PILCH	PARR
W. PILCH	SEWELL

MATCHES TO COME.

Thursday, July 1st, at Eton, the Marylebone Club against the Gentlemen of Eton.

Monday, July 5th, at Lord's, the Marylebone Club and Ground against the Bury and Suffolk Club.

Thursday, July 8th, at Lord's, the Marylebone Club and Ground against the Undergraduates of Oxford. Return Match.

Monday, July 12th, at Lord's, the Marylebone Club and Ground against the Cambridge Town and County Club

Thursday, July 15th, at Kennington Oval, the Marylebone Club and Ground against the County of Surrey. Return Match.

Saturday, July 17th, at Harrow, the Marylebone Club against the Gentlemen of Harrow

Monday, July 19th, at Lord's, the Gentlemen against the Players

Monday, July 26th, at Lord's, a Grand Match in honor of A. Mynn, Esq.

Wednesday, July 28th, Thursday, July 29th Friday, July 30th, & Saturday, July 31st, the Annual Matches between the Gentlemen of Harrow, Eton, and Winchester.

DARK's newly-invented Leg Guards.

Also his TUBULAR and other INDIA-RUBBER GLOVES, SPIKED SOLES

Bill poster advertising Kent *v.* England at Lord's, 1847.

girth. Mynn and Felix played their last Gentlemen and Players match at Lord's in 1852. The Lion of Kent (to give Mynn his other *nom de plume*) was over 6ft tall and he weighed nearly 18 stone. William Denison once said of Alfred Mynn: 'It was considered one of the grandest sights in cricket to see him advance and deliver the ball'. Most authorities would concur with the assertion that he was the greatest all-rounder before the advent of W.G. Grace.

Another great stalwart of the Kent team was the celebrated Fuller Pilch. He originally was one of the considerable number of fine cricketers to have originated from Norfolk. He had a baptism of fire when he made his first appearance at Lord's. Playing for his native county against MCC in 1820 he had of necessity to spend most of his time out in the field as William Ward amassed his monumental and record-breaking score of 278.

Fuller Pilch was a great stylist who used his height to considerable effect. He turned out for the Players at Lord's between 1827 and 1849 as well as for Kent from 1836 until 1854.

One other player ought to be mentioned: Herbert Jenner, who afterwards was to become better known as Herbert Jenner-Fust. His playing days were of an earlier period but he lived until 1904, when he died in his ninety-ninth year. He first appeared at Lord's in the 1822

Caricature of R.A. Fitzgerald by Alfred Gish Bryan (1852-1899).

The ground was used for more than sport – this photograph shows the Armoury of the West Middlesex Rifles in the 1860s.

Alfred Mynn, the 'Lion of Kent', by William Bromley.

Eton *v.* Harrow fixture and he captained Cambridge in the original Varsity match of 1827. He played for the Gentlemen *v.* Players from 1827 until 1836. He was President of MCC in 1833. Younger people used to hold the club's highest office in those days. In his prime he was the finest amateur cricketer in the entire country. His forte was wicket keeping. His professional life was spent as a barrister and thus his playing days were of but a limited duration, although he retained a very great interest in the game throughout the whole of his long life. His portrait can be seen at Lord's. He was certainly more at home there than dealing with his most celebrated case – this was the famous Gorham Judgement and dealt with the complicated issue as to whether a Devon vicar was heretical in his views on baptismal regeneration. Sir Herbert was widely felt to be out of his depth in this theological minefield.

A sketch of the Old Pavilion.

This famous painting by Henry Barraud (1811-1874) shows MCC members outside the pavilion at Lord's. Included in the group are the Prince of Wales (21st from the left) and W.G. Grace (38th from the left). The pavilion replaced the old building destroyed by fire in 1825.
(Museum of London.)

four

1866 – 1898

AN AGE OF GRACE

W.G. Grace in 1890 by Archibald Stuart-Wortley (1849-1905).

With MCC at long last firmly master of its own ground, progress became very rapid, both on and off the field. In the off-season of 1866/67, the original grandstand was built to the designs of Arthur Allom. (His descendant, Maurice J.C. Allom, was to take over the Presidency of MCC in 1969/70.) A year later the famous Tavern was erected. The architect was Edward Paraire. During the following summer the very first overseas touring team came to England in the guise of the Australian Aboriginal side. Members of the visiting team used a curious implement called a nulla-nulla in order to entertain the crowds during the intervals. This reminder of a great pioneering venture is still preserved in the museum at Lord's. In the same year R.A. Fitzgerald's appointment as Secretary of MCC became a salaried one. One feels that he highly deserved what was offered to him – the princely sum of £400 per annum.

An interesting sidelight on Fitzgerald's robust character can be observed in his astute handling of a major problem that arose four years later in 1872. He wanted very much to take an all-amateur side to North America, but surprising to say, this aroused the strong opposition of Mr Gladstone's government which was having great difficulties with the USA authorities over the Alabama incident. This was a hangover from the American Civil War. Fitzgerald, in his reply to the powers that were, explained that the proposed tour was a private venture, although he stated that he would be sorry to add to the difficulties which the government was undergoing at the time. The tour went ahead regardless and the whole trip was considered by those who were qualified to assess it to be a great success. Moreover, it introduced to the wider cricketing world and to the international scene two promising cricketers who would be heard of frequently in the future. They were W.G. Grace and the Hon. George (later Lord) Harris. The scrapbook that Fitzgerald kept whilst he was on the tour is preserved in the MCC Library. In addition a similar volume is kept in the archives of Brasenose College, Oxford. C.J. Ottaway, a brilliant scholar-athlete

(who alas died at a very young age) compiled it. He was the C.B. Fry of his generation.

The 1870s proved indeed to be busy times at Lord's. In 1870, F.C. Cobden achieved a dramatic hat-trick when he took all of the three remaining Oxford wickets to enable Cambridge to win by 3 runs in the Varsity Match. By 1870 the membership of MCC had risen to 1,265 – this was well over double the 1850 figure. Alas, the year was also memorable for tragedy at Lord's. George Summers was injured by a ball hitting him on the cheek in a match between MCC and Nottinghamshire. Summers seemed well enough to return to Nottingham, but he died a few days later. MCC erected a stone to his memory which bore the following inscription:

Aboriginal cricketers visited Lord's in 1868.

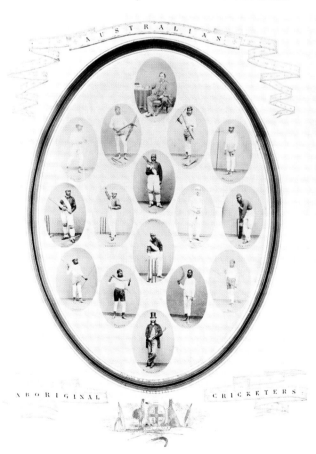

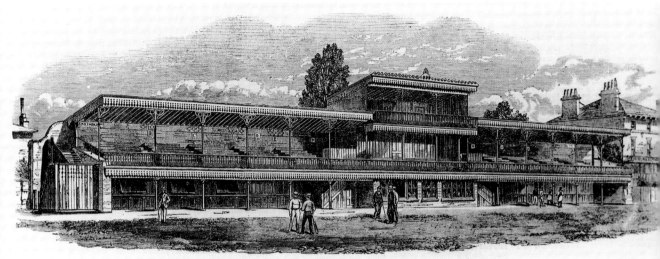

NEW GRAND STAND, LORD'S CRICKET-GROUND.

The new grandstand, 1867.

The ground, *c.* 1870.

The pavilion at Lord's, *c.* 1870.

Heavy roller and groundsmen, *c.* 1870.

The Laws of Lawn Tennis, published in 1876.

THIS TABLET IS ERECTED TO THE MEMORY
OF GEORGE SUMMERS BY THE MARYLEBONE
CRICKET CLUB TO MARK THEIR SENSE OF HIS
QUALITIES AS A CRICKETER AND TO TESTIFY
THEIR REGRET AT THE UNTIMELY INCIDENT
ON LORD'S GROUND WHICH CUT SHORT A
CAREER SO FULL OF PROMISE, JUNE 19th 1870
IN THE 26th YEAR OF HIS AGE.

Another sad loss, although less tragic, was the death of J.H. Dark on 17 October 1871 at the age of seventy-six. Alfred D. Taylor said that he had perhaps 'done more for MCC than any other individual'. Also in 1871, turnstiles were introduced to Lord's. Oxford won the Varsity match that year, S.E. Butler taking all 10 Cambridge wickets in the first innings for just 38 runs.

In 1874 there was even a baseball game played on the hallowed turf. The following year, the MCC Tennis and Rackets Sub-Committee were responsible for drawing up the first rules for the new game of lawn tennis. The influence of MCC in this sphere, it is sad to have to relate, rapidly diminished when the croquet club down at Wimbledon began to develop their own tournament. Even so, in the early days of the All England Lawn Tennis and Croquet Club, play would stop in the tournament for the duration of the Eton v. Harrow match at Lord's!

It is instructive to read the generous (but perhaps not undeserved) tribute which the author of *Tennis* (The Badminton Library) accords to MCC:

'They had to evolve order out of chaos, to formulate principles from imperfect analogies, and, with scanty experience to guide them to create a game. The code of the Marylebone Club was issued in 1875 and though soon superseded, for the moment it served its purpose, which could not have been attained by any less authoritative organisation, of bringing into harmony a variety of discordant methods.'

Not all members agreed, however, with the introduction of lawn tennis. At the 1875 Annual General Meeting of MCC, Mr Willoughby objected strongly to this innovation and ended an impassioned speech with 'a few words of advice to the Secretary, that if he wished to persuade the members to take a more active part in the game, a little more politeness would conduce to that desired object'. Another member to complain about Fitzgerald's manner was Dr Gaye, who had applied to the Secretary for permission for a band of Clown Cricketers to play at Lord's on behalf of a charitable corporation, but who had received an answer that he thought was 'scarcely polite'. Clearly Mr Fitzgerald's mental health was not as robust as it once was.

With all of these important goings on, it is probable that not many of the great names at Lord's took much notice of the arrival of a young lad in 1873 to work in the real tennis court. His name was Richard Gaby and he was the founder of the only dynasty at Lord's that over the years has been able to rival the Dark family. 100 years later in 1973, presentations were made to his sons G.M. (Joe, the head pavilion attendant) and R.T. (Dick Junior, the Club Superintendent) to celebrate a century of loyal and distinguished service that had been given to MCC by members of the Gaby family.

The Eton v. Harrow matches were social highlights of their respective seasons. Unfortunately, boys will be boys and the behaviour of the young gentlemen sometimes left a lot to be desired. The *Manchester Guardian* for 15 July 1873 loftily reported:

'The Eton v. Harrow match has this year proved, no doubt, a highly profitable affair for the proprietors of Lord's Cricket Ground; but there the profit ends, it is difficult to say which is most (sic) painful – the fulsome slang in which the *Daily Telegraph* gloats through three columns over the incidents of the great "event" or the disgraceful fight of excited schoolboys with which this match concluded.'

More notice at the time will certainly have been given to the resignation of R.A. Fitzgerald. His mental health had been giving cause for considerable concern for quite

Middlesex XI, 1878.

some period before this happened, but of his very great contribution to the development of Lord's, the club and of cricket in general there can be no doubt whatsoever. Fitzgerald was a good writer and, in common with his successor, he was a barrister. One of the very first signs of Mr Perkins' stewardship was the fact that in 1877 (the year after his appointment as Secretary of MCC) the Middlesex County Cricket Club pitched its tent – or rather its wickets – at Lord's. The county's previously nomadic existence was mercifully at an end and a memorable partnership with MCC was formed at Lord's. The regular provision of county cricket henceforth at the headquarters of cricket gave both the ground and its fixture list a staple diet.

The Middlesex County Cricket Club had been founded back in 1864. Their first ground was in the Islington Cattle Market Enclosure, but unfortunately there were very frequent rows and disputes with the landlord. It was with great relief that in the autumn of 1868 Middlesex made the decision to give up the tenancy. The following winter they turned down several overtures which MCC had made to them to encourage them to move into Lord's. 'Homeless and Houseless' (to quote the apt words of Lillywhite's *Cricketers' Companion*), they played but two games in 1869, both of them against Surrey. One of these

matches was played at Lord's. A couple of matches against that county were all that Middlesex could manage to play in the following two seasons as well.

In 1870, however, the county found a new home at Lillie Bridge in West Brompton on the Amateur Athletic Club running ground. This was hardly what one could describe as a success. At the County's Annual General Meeting, which was held on 18 July 1871, there was even the heretical suggestion made that there was not really room for a Middlesex XI in London – which already played host to MCC and to Surrey. Only 13 members attended this vital meeting and the defeatist motion was only overturned by a single vote. At the meeting, P.M. Thornton became Honorary Secretary of Middlesex CCC, a position that he was to hold with great devotion until 1899. Under Mr Thornton's wise guidance the affairs of Middlesex improved somewhat and at the AGM, which was held on 9 February 1872, it was decided to move to Prince's Ground in Hans Place, Kensington.

Middlesex stayed at Prince's until the end of the 1876 season. In the meantime, however, they had turned down a proposal that they should move to Alexandra Park and in addition they did not entertain another offer, which MCC made in 1875, that they should move to Lord's. At the end of the 1876 season, however, the position radically changed. The Middlesex officials had a very serious disagreement with the proprietors of Prince's over various matters of a financial nature. An Extraordinary General Meeting was therefore called on 7 November 1876 to discuss proposals from Mr Perkins, the Secretary of MCC. Even at this very late stage in the proceedings, there were to be found some who still had considerable reservations as to the wisdom of moving to the headquarters of cricket. The Middlesex captain of the time, I.D. Walker, in particular had his doubts about the financial viability of the scheme. Many of the members of Middlesex were in all probability swayed by Mr Thornton's insistence that the move be made forthwith. He stated that he would not continue in his post unless the club went to Lord's. At first the county club were in the fortunate position of paying nothing for the privilege of being based and of playing at Lord's. All good things have to come to an end, however, and in 1885 Middlesex began to make a financial contribution to MCC. Since 1899 a definite commercial arrangement has been in force between the two clubs.

In 1877 Test Cricket had its origin in Melbourne. The following year the very first expatriate Australian side came to visit England. They caused a great sensation in May 1878 by demolishing a very strong MCC side (which included W.G. Grace) in just over four and a half hours. This was in large measure due to their 'demon' bowler, F.R. Spofforth. The Australians bowled out the home side twice within the space of a single day. Never in the future would anyone at Lord's (or anywhere else in this country for that matter) be tempted to underestimate Antipodean cricketers. As a contemporary wrote:

The Australians came down like a wolf on the fold
When our Marylebone cracks for a trifle were bowled
When our Grace before dinner was very soon done
And our Grace after dinner did not score a run.

Another event in 1878, which was also very significant in its own less dramatic way, was the appointment of Sir Spencer Ponsonby-Fane as the Treasurer of MCC.

The touring Australians, photographed in 1878.

The founders of I Zingari, from left to right: Sir Spencer
Ponsonby-Fane, the Earl of Bessborough and J.L. Baldwin.

This position usually made its holder the *éminence grise* of Lord's. This is certainly what Sir Spencer very rapidly became at MCC. He was a retired diplomat and one of his most useful and long lasting roles was to help to found the club's historical collection. When MCC obtained the freehold in the 1860s they acquired some paintings. These were to help to form the nucleus of what is sometimes regarded as being the oldest sporting museum in the world. With his brother (the Earl of Bessborough) and his friend, J.L. Baldwin, Sir Spencer also founded the famous 'wandering' club of I Zingari. Sir Spencer was to remain as Treasurer at Lord's for a record thirty-seven years until 1915. By this latter date the world (both cricketing and otherwise) was in a very different state.

The tempo of change did not begin to slacken in the decade of the 1880s. One member, the Hon. Robert Grimston, however, almost certainly resented this. He became President in 1882 but, alas, he has the unique 'distinction' of being the only person to fail to survive his year of office. He was a very devoted supporter of cricket at his alma mater, Harrow School, but in other ways he was a die-hard traditionalist. He was universally reputed to have had an equal aversion to the introduction of lawnmowers into cricket grounds and to the legalisation of over-arm bowling – the latter having occurred in 1864. One issue of which Mr Grimston would most probably have approved, however, was the building of the Members' luncheon room in 1881.

Lord's was very slow off the mark in staging Test cricket. As we have already seen, contests between England and Australia were inaugurated at Melbourne back in 1877. The earliest Test matches on English soil were staged at Kennington Oval and at Old Trafford. The authorities at Lord's (with some considerable reason) took a very strong dislike to the way they understood the Australian crowds had treated Lord Harris and his team during the 1878/79 tour Down Under. MCC has recently published the diary that was kept by a young member of that team, Mr (later Revd) Vernon Royle. He had recently graduated from

Lord Harris, as drawn by Spy, the pseudonym of Sir Leslie Ward (1851-1922).

W.G. Grace and his contemporaries from the *Boy's Own Paper*, 1880.
Note the colourful cricketing dress of the period.

Brasenose College, Oxford, and he related with unselfconscious delight his experiences – these included seeing an electric light for the first time as he returned to England via the United States.

As a result of the ill feeling which had been generated on the 1878/79 tour, there was no very great enthusiasm on MCC's part to stage an international match at Lord's when an Australian side came to these shores in 1880. Indeed, the visiting Antipodeans had no fixture at the headquarters of cricket during their tour. In the event it was Lord Harris himself who felt that there was a clear and demonstrable need to bury the hatchet and so he joined forces with Mr C.W. Alcock – the innovative Secretary of Surrey County Cricket Club – to stage at The Oval the first ever Test match on English soil. Mr Alcock was one of the relatively unsung heroes of Victorian sport. In addition to being the virtual founder of Test cricket in England, he was the driving force behind the establish-

ment of the FA Cup. He was also a magistrate, a distinguished author and the editor of *Cricket: A Weekly Record of the Game*. This invaluable journal first appeared in 1882; Mr Alcock was quite clearly a workaholic.

The arrangements which were needed to stage the Test match at The Oval took quite a considerable time, as these things tend to do. As a result the game did not happen until September. By this time, as Lord Harris observed in his autobiography, several England players were not available to be selected on account of their presence on the country's grouse moors! The famous Test match in 1882 when Australia defeated England for the first time on home soil, thus giving rise to the obituary notice that created the Ashes saga, also took place at The Oval. The

The Ashes urn pictured alongside the Ashes Cup.

Charles Alcock.

W.G. Grace and the England XI, 1886. England won all three
encounters with the Australians that year.

opening Test match in 1884 was played up at Old Trafford
and so it was not until later on in that season that Lord's
had the honour of staging an international match for the
very first time. In this game England defeated the old (or
rather young at this stage) enemy by an innings. Fresh
horizons for international cricket were also opened up in
1886. That year witnessed the arrival of the Parsees. These
were the first tourists to come to England from India, the
supreme jewel in Queen Victoria's imperial crown.

With the theme of empire in mind, we come to 1887. This
was a most notable year both parochially and internationally.
It was most appropriate that what was regarded as being the
most imperial of all games should be holding the centenary
of its premier club in the very same year that Queen Victoria
was celebrating her Golden Jubilee. So far as Lord's and
MCC were concerned, the most lasting result of the celebrations was the purchase of the adjacent Henderson's Nursery.
This once famous market garden has given its name to that
evocative expression 'the Nursery End'. By a marvellous piece
of serendipity the market garden nursery has, in the course of
time, become the nursery for training young cricketers.

The Parsees touring team of 1886 – the first Indian representative side
to play in England and at Lord's.

A colour lithograph of Henderson's nursery, c.1857,
by Ben George. (City of Westminster Archive.)

An imaginary cricket match between England and Australia, 1887. This was
painted by Sir Robert Ponsonby Staples and George Hamilton Barrable.
Lillie Langtry (right foreground) is tactfully averting her gaze as the Prince
and Princess of Wales approach (apparently walking on the field of play in
the middle of an over).

Lord's cricket ground, 1887.

In order to celebrate the centenary of MCC there was held a special dinner in the capacious premises of the old tennis court. A 'perfect' dinner was provided and the band of the 'S' Division of the Metropolitan Police played an excellent selection of music during the meal. There were many speeches – possibly too many for the likes of some – including contributions from the Chancellor of the Exchequer, the French Ambassador and the Lord Chamberlain. Sir Saul Samuel was the speaker who was chosen to respond 'on behalf of the colonies'. He made in the course of his speech a remark which was doubtless typical of its time but which nevertheless is not at all likely to be heard these days – 'All Australians regarded them-selves as Englishmen'. Dr W.G. Grace was the obvious per-son to speak on behalf of the medical profession for the kind way in which all had spoken of him. 'WG' was a man of few words; public speaking was not at all his forte.

This life-size bust of W.G. Grace (dating from 1888) was presented to MCC by Mrs Grace in 1919.

The pace of events at cricket's headquarters showed no signs of slackening as the decade drew to its close. In 1889 the old pavilion was demolished. It had for some time been deemed to be clearly inadequate for the accommodation of the increased membership of MCC. To judge from the evidence which is afforded by contemporary illustrations, it looked rather like an Indian railway station of the period. The best impression of the old pavilion that one can find is to be discovered in the painting by Henry Barraud. This well-known picture is part of the collection that is housed at the Museum of London.

Thomas Verity was the architect who was chosen to carry out the important work of designing the new pavilion. He had had some considerable input into the designs for the Royal Albert Hall and also for the Criterion development at Piccadilly Circus. Mr Verity was thus an established and an experienced professional in his field but he was not, however, to be without his share of headaches, which hampered him as he endeavoured to carry out his prestigious commission. Verity had the intention of constructing a building that was made of stone, but it seems that there was a strike by the masons at the time. The architect had therefore to compromise and to construct instead the brick and terracotta edifice that is known and loved by cricketers all over the world. The new pavilion was opened on 1 May 1890. It contains at its heart the famous Long Room – the Mecca of cricketers far and wide. The speed with which this very fine building was erected was truly remarkable. The old pavilion was standing for the last match of the 1889 season. The new replacement was all ready by the beginning of the following May. One very endearing feature of the design is the series of rain stops, which, rather in the manner of medieval gargoyles, take the form of caricatures of members of the MCC Committee of the time.

An engraving of Thomas Verity's design for the new pavilion, 1889. Note the coach-and-four emerging from the archway.

The new pavilion, 1890. The noble proportions of the new building seem
even finer unencroached with adjacent structures as they are now.

William Nicholson, the generous benefactor of Lord's.

At the Annual General Meeting of MCC the Committee reported:

'Acting in accordance with the rules of the club, the committee have made no permanent arrangement for paying the cost of the new pavilion by mortgage or charging the property of the club; a certain sum has been paid out of the income of 1889 and 1890 and the remainder has been borrowed from the club's bankers from time to time to meet the architect's certificates.

'A sum of money over and above what can be conveniently paid from the current income of the past and present years will be required. Mr Nicholson has generously offered to advance this sum as a temporary loan on favourable terms, an offer which the committee have decided to accept.'

The pavilion was for a time nicknamed 'The Gin Palace', because the family fortunes of the generous Mr William Nicholson had very largely come from the sales of that beverage. MCC was indeed very fortunate to have such a generous benefactor. They also showed very good judgement in accepting the designs that Mr Verity submitted. A sketch by Mr R. Creed FRIBA was quite recently discovered at Lord's in the pavilion basement, where it had been gathering much dust for over 100 years. It is dated 25 February 1889 and it was Mr Creed's unsuccessful submission of his design for the new pavilion. So far as one can judge it would have made an uninspiring building. Mr Creed was, however, in general a very competent man. The Leyton Cricket Ground was made under his superintendence on part of the Lyttelton estate in 1883. A contemporary report says that the ground 'gave unwonted loveliness to a district which but a short time since presented an appearance of the abomination of desolation'.

As we come to leave the decade of the 1880s we may pause for a moment to observe a humbler scene. On 20 May 1887 (the year when MCC celebrated its centenary) a young lad who had but very recently arrived from the West Indies visited the ground for the first time. His name was Pelham Warner; his father had been born two days before the Battle of Trafalgar was fought and his son (the future Sir Pelham or 'Plum' as he was almost universally known) was to live until 1963. This was the year of the inauguration of the Gillette Cup. Plum Warner was never to forget the very first wicket that he saw at Lord's. The great actor, C. Aubrey Smith, clean bowled the future MCC Secretary, F.E. Lacey. Both of these remarkable men were eventually to receive a knighthood, as was their juvenile spectator.

Warner gives a vivid picture of the ground at this (from our present vantage point) halfway mark in its history.

'How different was Lord's then from what it is today! Only three buildings remain [Warner was writing in 1946] – Block A, on the left of the pavilion as one looks at the wickets, the hotel and the members' luncheon room. The present pavilion was not built until 1890. There was no big scoreboard or "Father Time"; the stands were few and small, and there was nothing like the seating capacity we are accustomed to in these days. The Northern end of the "Nursery" had only just been purchased by the MCC, but the atmosphere was the same then as now. Lord's was the home and the headquarters of cricket, with a tradition and history which no other ground in the world ever quite succeeded in capturing.'

Warner gives a good pen picture of the ground at this date and two famous pictures also help us to visualise the place. In 1887, George Hamilton Barrable and Sir Robert Ponsonby Staples painted a celebrated panoramic view of Lord's during an imaginary match between England and Australia. Grace is depicted batting, whilst the Prince and Prince of Wales can be observed walking along the boundary in the middle of an over. At least Lillie Langtry is tactfully averting her gaze so as not to see this breach of cricketing etiquette. The painting gives one the best impressions of the second pavilion at Lord's (which was soon to be demolished) and of the capacious tennis court (which also had only a few more years to go). The Tavern is the other building that is clearly visible in the painting.

The Eton *v.* Harrow match of 1886. This fine painting is by Albert Chevallier Tayler (1862-1925) and shows the old 'A' enclosure and pavilion.

Gentlemen *v*. Players at Lord's by Sir Robert Ponsonby Staples (1853-1943).
W.G. Grace can be seen in the pavillion enclosure. Note the professionals
leaving from a separate entrance.

Eton *v.* Harrow, c. 1889 by Albert Ludovici Jnr (1852-1932).

The real tennis court is even more clearly seen in Archibald Stuart-Wortley's celebrated portrait of W.G. Grace. The sitter not surprisingly took a keen interest in the arrangements for this composition. A letter survives from Grace to Harry Perkins, the MCC Secretary, in which he said 'I think a small size would spoil the whole thing'. A large painting indeed is what resulted – W.G. Grace was no shrinking violet!

The commissioning of the portrait is best told in the words of the MCC Minutes for 21 July 1890.

'By a resolution of Committee… a notice was ordered to be posted in the Pavilion inviting a subscription limited to £1 by Members of the Club in order that a portrait of Mr W.G. Grace might be painted and eventually hung in the Pavilion.

'Mr A. Stuart-Wortley was commissioned to execute the portrait which has been completed to the satisfaction of the sub-committee and is now being exhibited at the Royal Academy. The subscription list reached the sum of £400 and there may be some few more subscriptions to come in – of this £350 has been paid to Mr Wortley for the portrait and copyright thereof and the balance will cover the expenses connected with it.'

If Mr Henry Perkins, the Secretary of MCC, was ever tempted to rest on his laurels as the ground and the club started to enter the decade of the 1890s, he was soon to be totally disabused. The Manchester, Sheffield & Lincolnshire Railway wanted to extend their operations into the very heart of London and Lord's cricket ground was quite literally in their way! After heated correspondence and stormy public meetings had been conducted, the more sober work of negotiation had to be taken in hand. There are bulging files of papers that have been preserved at the Public Record Office in Kew. These documents give one a very clear idea of the story from the railway company's point of view. In the end, honour was satisfied on both sides but it had been a close-run thing. MCC acquired the site of the adjacent Clergy Orphanage in exchange for granting the railway company the right to dig under a part of the

practice ground. Lord's was saved by a whisker – or rather by a tunnel! The boys of the Clergy Orphanage moved to Canterbury to form the public school at St Edmund's, whilst the girls were to become the nucleus of St Margaret's in Bushey.

The drama over the Nursery end was rather intense and very protracted. The position was summed up as well as anywhere in a letter, dated 11 December 1890, from Mr C. Liddell (an engineer) to Mr W. Pollitt of the railway company:

'I have seen Mr Perkins and after a full explanation he explained his determination to oppose the line to the utmost – he says the committee have paid £25,000 for 3 acres of the nursery grounds and that they don't want to sell any part… and will do their utmost to prevent the Manchester Sheffield & Lincolnshire Company taking a foot of their ground. In short he is irreconcilable.'

On the same day a large public meeting was held in the recently built pavilion at Lord's to register a very robust and vigorous protest against the proposed railway scheme. Mr Seager Hunt MP was in the chair and a veritable army of distinguished artists, ecclesiastics and local politicians lent their support to him.

The girls of the Clergy Orphanage.

Gentleman v. Players at Lord's, painted in 1895 by Dickinsons. The teams
shown did not actually play, but the players are largely notable names of
that time. From left to right: J. Phillips (umpire), A. Ward, A.E. Stoddart and
W.G. Grace (batsmen), J.T. Hearne, G.A. Lohmann, W. Gunn, A. Shrewsbury,
R. Peel, R. Briggs, J. Wheeler (umpire), J.M. Read, W.H. Lockwood
and W. Attewell.

W.G. Grace as drawn by George Elgar Hicks (1824-1914).

There is a memorandum, dated 16 December 1890, which has been preserved at the Public Record Office. In it one can find the statement that Mr Pollitt sent on behalf of the railway company and met the Secretary of MCC.

'Mr Perkins expressed himself very strongly against the slightest interference with the cricket ground. He said that they had for years been steadily improving their position and had now got a freehold property which had cost them about £100,000, that they were not a dividend-paying concern, their only object being to enable the public to see the finest cricket for 6d each.'

The following month Mr Perkins sought to further his campaign with a circular letter which was addressed to the secretaries of cricket clubs and other organisations in London in which he objected to the 'wanton and unnec-

essary interference' with Lord's. This was succeeded in its turn with a letter to *The Times* of 30 January 1901, in which some officials of the railway company attempted to contradict Mr Perkins.

The first hint of a possible compromise is contained in a letter which was sent on 11 February 1891 from Mr S. Bircham (the solicitor acting for MCC) to Sir Theodore

W.G. Grace as drawn by Spy.
The watercolour featured in *Vanity Fair*.

This banquet held at Clifton was one of the many celebrations to mark W.G. Grace's 100th century.

W.G. Grace wearing his MCC cap.
The caricature was drawn by Alfred Gish Bryan.

Martin in which it is mentioned that the club was offered an area of ground from the adjacent Clergy Orphanage School which was double in extent to that to be taken by the railway company. Sir Theodore Martin wasted no time in taking action. He followed this letter up with his own epistle which he wrote to Mr Liddell the same day:

'Herewith I send a copy of the terms stipulated by the Lord's people. They are very stiff, but I fear they will stand to them.'

On 20 February agreement was at long last reached. On 11 February 1891 the *Manchester Courier* hinted that a compromise might be reached. It opined that the inhabitants of St John's Wood had been 'left in the lurch by the cricketers', although it conceded that it was possible that the 'working classes of Marylebone' would 'welcome the idea of a great railway terminus in the district'.

Various meetings were held at Lord's to tie up the matter. On 8 December 1891 there was held a very large gathering of MCC members. Mr Bircham, the solicitor, wrote:

'The Committee were unanimous as to the course which would be adopted in record to the position to be assumed by the club… but it was evident that there was a very divided feeling among members of the club generally.'

One dissenting member of MCC wrote to *Horse & Hound* and signed himself 'No Surrender'.

In the event, Clause 3 of Section 52 of the Extension to London Line Act gave specific protection to MCC. One condition was that the railway company should ensure that the tunnelling and covered way digging should only affect a portion of the practice ground and that, when the work was completed, this new portion should show no difference to the old.

On 31 August, Sir Francis Fox, the great engineer, reported (with, no doubt, a great sigh of relief) that the contractors had gained entry into Lord's. On 13 May of the following year he wrote to Mr Pollitt: 'I hear such general commendation from the members of the MCC concerning the work in progress.' Finally, on 6 April 1895,

he told Mr Pollitt 'The work in connection with this cricket ground is now completed, the wall being built and the siding lay down.'

Marylebone Station was the last of the great London termini to be built and it very nearly became the first to close. Sir Edward Watkin, Bart MP (the Victorian railway chairman) was a man who was in many respects a person who was ahead of his time. He was, for example, an early exponent of the Channel tunnel. He viewed Marylebone as being merely a link between his railway lines and important routes to the South Coast, as well as, via the tunnel, to the Continent of Europe. He unfortunately had a stroke in 1894, shortly after he gained agreement for the main points of his extension of the line into Marylebone. It was thus to be his successor, Lord Wharncliffe, who was to be the one with the opportunity of bringing the scheme to completion.

The Great Central Railway was not, however, flushed with funds. It is believed that money was not available to enable the company to employ an architect to design Marylebone Station, and so this work was entrusted to a member of their engineering staff. The tunnel project had

Tunnelling work being carried out on the Nursery in December 1896, to allow the railway line to extend to Marylebone.

Sir Francis Lacey, Secretary of MCC, at the end of the nineteenth century.

The ground in 1898.

The 1898 Varsity Match during the luncheon interval.

quite clearly stretched the company's resources. This perhaps explains the rather quaint and homely appearance of the station building. The first train to leave Marylebone Station departed in March 1899.

It is very pleasant to be able to report that relations nowadays between the club and the railway authorities are much more cordial. At the time of the centenary of the dispute, MCC officials were entertained to a champagne breakfast and the club was presented with the last semaphore signal to have been used at a mainline London terminus.

This episode was to represent Henry Perkins' finest hour. A less satisfactory episode occurred at the Lord Chamberlain's office on 25 January 1892. For some reason, an MCC committee meeting was held in these august surroundings. On this occasion the club was offered a 'library of cricket works'. This was turned down with the note 'Declined – for the present at any rate'. This unfortunate decision would seem to have marked a reversal of previous committee policy. In 1884, to take one instance, we read in the minutes that 'an estimate from Whelpdale for the bookcases for the members' room was accepted'.

On 20 July 1893, however, a certain Captain H.B. Sutherland presented the various volumes from the Badminton Library to MCC with hope that other members may do likewise. These books still survive and form the nucleus of a famous collection of cricketing literature. Subsequent additions have come from many sources and these have included items from the well-known Ford, Ashley-Cooper and Cahn collections. These have all made their contribution to make the MCC Library into a reference collection with few rivals in the world of cricket.

Captain Sutherland (the original benefactor) was a cricketer who had played for Eton. He subsequently turned out for Cheshire and for Kent. Many better-known practitioners of the game have not done nearly so much for cricket as Captain Sutherland achieved by his generous gift to Lord's.

If the victory over the railway company represented the greatest triumph of Henry Perkins, the *annus mirabilis* for Dr W.G. Grace undoubtedly occurred in 1895 when he completed the previously unknown feats of scoring 1,000 runs in May and in addition of reaching his hundredth century. There were also great festivities on 18 July 1898 when he celebrated his fiftieth birthday. The Gentlemen *v.* Players match was commenced on that day and every player who took part in that match was presented by MCC with a medal that had been specifically struck in honour of the occasion. Film footage of this great event still survives and it was shown on the big screen to the spectators (who included many descendants of W.G. Grace) who came to Lord's exactly 100 years later to the day on 18 July 1998 for the commemoration of the 150th anniversary of the great man's birth.

1898 was also notable in that it was the year in which Henry Perkins, the Secretary of MCC, retired. He was succeeded by an even greater man in the person of Francis Lacey – a fellow barrister who was to become the first cricketer to receive a knighthood for his services to the game. Perkins is reputed to have given his successor this immortal (or is it immoral?) piece of advice: 'Lacey, on no account whatsoever should you take any notice of the… Committee!'

five

1898 – 1926

WAR AND PEACE

Arthur Trott as depicted by Albert Chevallier Tayler (1862-1925).

Francis Lacey in more ways than one brought Lord's and MCC into the twentieth century. Almost from the very moment that he arrived at the headquarters of cricket, work was commenced on extensive building operations. The real tennis court was moved and in its place the first Mound Stand was erected; 200 life members were elected in 1900 at £200 each in order to pay for the latter building. The old tennis court can be seen, as we have noticed, in the background of Archibald Stuart-Wortley's famous 1890 portrait of the Champion. The court was relocated to its present site behind the pavilion. Real tennis started afresh in its new surroundings with great panache on 1 January.

In 1899 Albert Trott, an Australian who played for Middlesex, was to achieve immortality (when appearing for MCC against the Australians) by hitting a ball for a six, clean over the pavilion; a stupendous achievement that has never again been repeated. The bat with which he achieved this great feat is now on display in the MCC Museum. In 1907 he was to perform a further

Arthur Trott.

The old tennis court at Lord's in 1899. It was demolished shortly afterwards.

Soldiers at Lord's during the Boer War, *c.* 1900.

A lunch interval, *c.* 1900.

MCC's first official touring team, led by Sir Pelham Warner, in Australia, 1903/04.

Plum Warner is chaired off the field having won the Championship in the dying moments of his last match, 1920.

F.E. Lacey by G. Spencer Watson.

unprecedented act, this time as a bowler. Playing for Middlesex against Sussex he took four wickets with four consecutive balls and in addition he performed the hat-trick in the same match. This brought the game to a rather premature halt to the considerable detriment of his benefit takings. It does not always pay in this life to be too successful…

Under Francis Lacey's lively and dynamic leadership at Lord's many changes of considerable significance were made at MCC. One of the most important had very humble origins. In 1901 a member enquired as to whether coaching facilities could be provided for his schoolboy son. The Secretary replied in due course to say that he was very ready to organise a net if five others would be prepared to join in the scheme. With the sanction of the MCC Committee the first class of six boys was held in the Easter holidays of 1902. From this very small acorn a mighty oak tree has sprung. Many well-known cricketers and others who are eminent today in public life are able to look back with gratitude to the Easter coaching classes which they attended in their salad days at Lord's.

Two of Lacey's schemes were to be but short lived. During the first weeks of the 1900 season MCC enclosed Lord's with a net two and a half feet in height. The idea was that the batsmen should run out their hits but the experiment was unsuccessful. It was first arranged that three runs should be scored when the ball went over the netting and two runs in addition to those which had already been run when it was stopped by the net. The innovation did not encourage big hits over the ropes and was adjudged to be altogether clumsy.

Another short-lived idea was the introduction of lacrosse to the headquarters of cricket. Lacrosse matches were played at Lord's in the early spring of 1903. *Wisden* said 'as the game is earning a well-merited popularity, it is probably [*sic*] that these matches will again be permitted'. Lacrosse is not a game with which Lord's is nowadays normally associated. However, a more lasting innovation was the first match at Lord's to be played by a representative

public schools team. The most important decision at Lord's came on 4 June that year when P.F. Warner was asked to captain the first official MCC touring team to Australia.

As a result of this decision the team went out down under sporting their new caps and blazers that bore the badge of St George and the dragon. (Later in the decade King Edward VII gave those playing for England at home the rare privilege of being able to use the royal arms of the crown and three lions.) One of Warner's team was B.J.T. Bosanquet. He was famous for inventing the googly (or the 'bosie' that the Australians named after him) but perhaps he is these days better known as the father of Reggie Bosanquet of television news fame. The diary which one of the team, R.E. Foster, kept on the tour has been preserved and is now on view in the MCC Museum. On the tour Foster made the then record Test match score of 187 at Sydney.

Francis Lacey was also instrumental in establishing the Advisory County Cricket Committee which had its initial meeting at Lord's in 1904. That year also saw a visit to the headquarters of cricket from the International Olympic Committee. This was probably due to the influence of Lord Desborough, who was prominent both at Lord's and in the Olympic movement. Indeed, there had been some token cricketing presence at the 1900 Paris Games and so perhaps Lord Desborough was anxious to try to make cricket an Olympic sport.

In 1906 a new press box was added to the facilities at Lord's. Previous accommodation for members of the Fourth Estate had met with much criticism. The following season the first Test matches in England took place against South Africa and in the same year there occurred Albert Trott's remarkable benefit match to which reference has already been made. Francis Lacey was also instrumental in convening in 1909 the first meeting of the Imperial Cricket Conference, which drew to its inaugural meeting delegates from England, Australia and South Africa. As a direct result of this consultation these three countries took part in a unique triangular tournament in 1912.

A wedding reception at the ground, 1907.

The match between Australia and South Africa that year was the only occasion when a Test match has been played at Lord's in which England has not taken part. The contest was largely the brainchild of the South African diamond millionaire Sir Abe Bailey, whose son was in later years to captain Gloucestershire.

The general feeling was that the Triangular Tournament was rather a disappointment. The weather was very bad during the summer of 1912, the Australian team was very unrepresentative due to a bitter dispute between the newly-formed Australian Board of Control and several of that country's leading cricketers and, to cap it all, the South Africans did not live up to the standard set by their great 1907 team.

Meanwhile back in 1910 there occurred the celebrated game that has gone down in history as Fowler's Match. This took place in the Eton *v.* Harrow fixture that year. When Eton followed on in their second innings they were only four runs ahead when the ninth wicket fell. There

then followed a very plucky last wicket stand of 50 runs in only 25 minutes but all the same the result of the match must have seemed to any rational spectator to be a foregone conclusion. In the second Harrow innings, however, R.St L. Fowler took eight wickets for only 23 runs. Eton were the victors by a margin of nine runs. Among the players on the losing Harrovian side were a future cabinet minister and a field marshal in the making. They were both in due course to become President of MCC. They were Lord Monckton of Brenchley and Lord Alexander of Tunis respectively. There were 5,219 members of MCC in 1910, an increase of over 1,500 on the 1890 figure.

1914 turned out to be a very unfortunate time in which to celebrate the centenary of the present Lord's Ground. There took place in that year a great dinner at the Hotel Cecil over which the great Yorkshire cricketer, Lord Hawke, took the chair and presided. The aging Dr W.G. Grace was given a great ovation when he rose to reply to the toast of the 'County Cricket Club'.

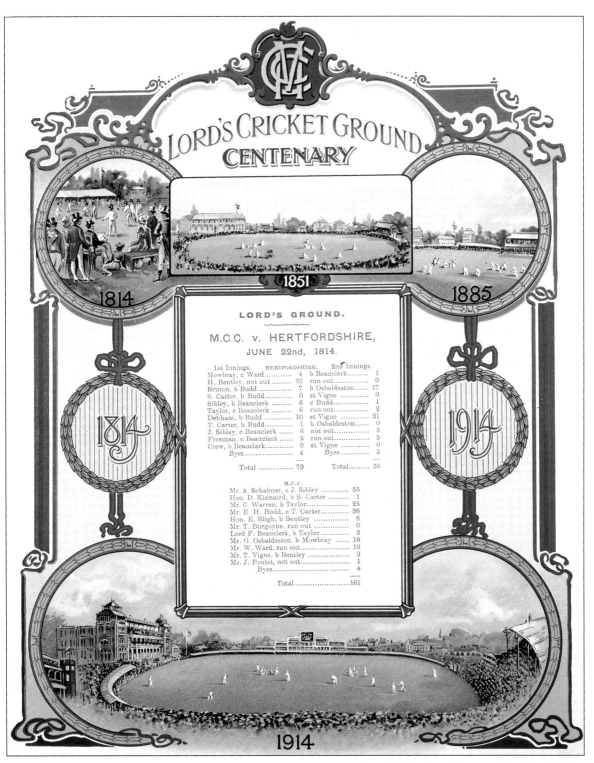

Lord's Cricket Ground Centenary Match Card, MCC *v.*
Hertfordshire, 22 June 1814 - 1914.

Programme for the 1914 Centenary Match between the MCC's South African team and The Rest.

Public speaking, as we have already noticed, was not really W.G.'s forte, but those who were present on that occasion seemed to have had a premonition that it was to be his swansong. It also in retrospect proved to mark the end of a golden age in the long history of our national game.

The same Sir Edward Grey who had won the MCC Gold Tennis Prize was to make as Foreign Secretary the famous remark at the onset of the Great War that the lights were going out all over Europe.

Before the fateful month of August 1914 had drawn to its melancholy close, many cricketers were engaged in a much grimmer conflict. The County Championship, however, went on its stately way undisturbed by the outbreak of a world war. This displeased W.G. Grace. He wrote prophetically (at a time when many people thought that the war would be over by Christmas) that he thought that the hostilities were likely to continue for a long time and he further ventured his considered opinion that it was not

at all proper that some young men were continuing to play cricket whilst others of their contemporaries were giving up their lives for their country.

Before the end of the year many fine young men had indeed died. One such was Captain A.E.J. Collins who had made the highest ever recorded score (628 not out) whilst playing in a house match at Clifton College in 1899.

Dr Grace died in the following year. His much lamented passing and the advent of a world war naturally symbolised for many the passing of an era. Indeed, *Wisden* for 1916 made for particularly melancholy reading. In addition to recording the deaths in action of so many young and heroic men, it paid tribute to W.G. As if that were not loss enough, Victor Trumper and A.E. Stoddart also had their obituary notices in the same volume. If it was indeed the end of an era, what an era it had been!

Possibly the best way in which one can sum up this period is to quote Sir Pelham Warner who knew personally all the cricketers involved:

'There are periods in all walks of life when great names abound, and in the history of English cricket we find such a period between 1895 and 1914. Among amateur batsmen, with Ranjitsinhji, Jackson, McClaren, Fry, Stoddart, O'Brien, A.O. Jones, Palairet, Jessop, H.K. Foster, R.E. Foster, Spooner, Perrin and Hutchings and, of course, W.G., there was a plethora of talent, which coincided with a great revival of fast bowling in Richardson, Mold, Lockwood, Kortright, Woodcock, Brearley, Hirst, Knox, Buckenham, Fielder, Gill, Bradley, Warren and Wass. Medium to fast bowlers included J.T. Hearne, S.F. Barnes, W. Mead, Poucher and A.E. Relf, and when the great slow left-handers Peel and Briggs dropped out, immediate successors were found in Rhodes and Blythe, followed later by Dean. Among all-rounders of the highest class were Mason, Rhodes, J.N. Crawford, C.L. Townsend, Arnold, Bosanquet, Braund, J.W.H.T. Douglas and F.R. Foster. Of professional batsmen Shrewsbury, William Gunn, Abel, Hayward, J.T. Tyldesley, Hobbs, Woolley, J.W. Hearne, P. Mead, George Gunn, J.T. Brown, Denton and W.G. Quaife stood out. In such an era of talent some of these found only a very occasional place in an England Eleven. So strong was amateur batting that the England teams at Lord's and at Birmingham against the Australians in 1902 included only one professional played solely for his batting – J.T. Tyldesley. All these cricketers were gifted with genius and personality, and a spectator had no need to consult the scorecard, he knew who was batting or bowling because of that player's outstanding individuality.'

Of those great names mentioned above by 'Plum' Warner, Charlie Blythe and K.L. Hutchings were among the most notable casualties of the First World War. They can be seen in A. Chevallier Tayler's great painting of Kent

v. Lancashire in 1906, which is on long-term loan to MCC from the St Lawrence County Cricket Ground, Canterbury. It is a very salutary experience to inspect the names on the First World War Memorial in the pavilion at Lord's. This lists all those members of MCC who are known to have perished in that savage conflict; for some very strange reason a similar memorial was not erected to commemorate those who were casualties of the Second World War. The roll for 1914-1918 is the more horrendous when one realises that MCC was a comparatively small club in those days. One holder of the Victoria Cross is commemorated on this memorial. He was Captain Francis Grenfell VC, an heroic member of a great sporting family.

MCC members gather at the Centenary Dinner in 1914.

J.T. Tyldesley, by Albert Chevallier Tayler.

K.S. Ranjitsinhji by Albert Chevallier Tayler.

Programme for the wartime baseball match played at Lord's in 1917 between the USA and Canada.

Lord's was taken over for use by various national bodies in the First World War. From time to time units of the Territorial Army, the Army Service Corps (Transport) and the Royal Army Medical Corps were in occupation of the ground, together with those who were attending classes in wireless instruction and in military cooking. The club's property at 2 Grove End Road was lent for the war effort and was used as the headquarters of the Royal Volunteer Battalion (London Regiment). After the war was over Francis Lacey received a thank you letter in January 1919 from the War Office. It read:

'I am commanded by the Army Council to ask you to convey to the members of your committee their deep appreciation of the patriotic action of the Marylebone Cricket Club in so promptly placing their ground and premises at Lord's at the disposal of the military authorities in August 1914. The Army Council consider that the use of your historic grounds for training purposes has been invaluable, especially in the case of those candidates for the King's Commission who have received their training in the very home of the great game which has done so much in producing that spirit of sportsmanship which is a tradition of the British officer. The Army Council also desire to thank you and your staff for the assistance which has been so readily given on every occasion.'

At first the only matches which were played on the sacred turf at Lord's during the early stages of the war were inter-service games. It did, however, remain the policy of the MCC Committee to continue to send sides around the country to play against the various public schools. In the long run, other activities were permitted including a baseball match that was staged in 1916 between Canadian soldiers and Americans in London. This game was played in order to raise money in aid of a fund that had been established to help the widows and children of Canadians who had been killed in action. The match even attracted royal spectators along with a galaxy of political and military notables.

Towards the end of the Great War, charity matches were introduced. In 1917 an English Army Eleven played an Australian Eleven. Among other fixtures, the Army and the Navy were pitted against the Australian and South African forces. In the following year, two matches were staged between England and the Dominions. Among those who witnessed the second match were HM King George V and HRH the Duke of Connaught.

At the Annual General Meeting of MCC in 1919, it was decided that it would be very appropriate to honour various war leaders. Admiral Viscount Jellicoe, Admiral Sir David Beatty, Field Marshal Viscount French and Field

Marshal Sir Douglas Haig were all made honorary members of the club. Another event which hit the headlines in 1919 was the appearance of G.T.S. Stevens for the Gentlemen against the Players whilst he was still a pupil at University College School.

In 1920 there were 5,568 members of MCC – a slight increase on the 1910 figure. In that year there took place one of the very great moments in the history of Lord's. 'Plum' Warner in his very last match was carried shoulder high off the ground in triumph after leading Middlesex to an exciting win in the local derby over Surrey amidst the twilight. By this achievement Middlesex were able to clinch the county championship for the first time since 1903 – another significant year in Warner's life. It was a superbly fitting end to the career of a great Lord's stalwart.

Three years later an even more eminent exponent of the game was commemorated at Lord's. The Grace Gates were opened in July 1923 in St John's Wood Road to serve as the members' entrance. The inscription reads:

TO THE

MEMORY OF

WILLIAM GILBERT GRACE

THE GREAT CRICKETER 1848-1915

THESE GATES WERE ERECTED BY THE M.C.C.

AND OTHER FRIENDS

AND ADMIRERS

The gates are a fine example of Worcestershire ironwork. Sir Herbert Baker, whose work is to be seen in several places around the ground, designed them.

The final months with Francis Lacey spent as Secretary of MCC were very busy ones for him. In preparation for the forthcoming visit of the Australian touring team, Sir Herbert Baker was pressed into service again. He designed a new grandstand, which was built in the off-season of 1925/26. The cost of this work was a mere £46,000. The committee may have been pleased to have had a new building which did not prove to be too much of a drain on the club's finances, but not everybody was impressed with the finished product. One influential critic was none other than 'Plum' Warner. In 1946 in a rare moment of criticism he parodied Sir Winston Churchill and wrote: 'Never in the history of cricket has so large a stand held so few people.'

Warner was clearly underwhelmed by the new grandstand. One of its defects consisted in the fact that too many seats afforded a restricted view. The architect, however, disarmed criticism by presenting to MCC Father Time which is possibly the most famous weathervane in the country – it is perhaps only rivalled by the grasshopper which surmounts the Royal Exchange building in the City of London. Father Time has successfully withstood a world war and the 1987 mini-hurricane. It is a very old piece of symbolism and in its non-cricketing guise it appears on the seventeenth-century pulpit in the Somerset parish church of Stoke St Gregory and also on the eighteenth-century weathervane of St Giles', Cripplegate. The latter is now housed in the Museum of London. Father Time was almost the only part of the fabric at Lord's to be damaged in the Second World War but he was very soon repaired. The weathervane had to be removed when Sir Herbert Baker's grandstand was demolished in 1998. It now adorns a commanding position on the other side of the ground on top of the lift shaft.

The Grace Gates.

The Australian team of 1921.

Reverting to the field of play, in September 1920 MCC sent a side to Australia under the captaincy of the redoubtable J.W.H.T. Douglas. It was in reality too soon after the war, but Australia had not seen an MCC team for nine years and large crowds turned out everywhere to watch the matches. The great Australian touring side of 1921 inevitably were victorious in the Lord's Test. The administration of the match was not up to Lord's usual high standards, however, and *Wisden* was not impressed:

'The arrangements for dealing with the crowd proved inadequate, many ticket-holders being greatly delayed and inconvenienced in getting through the gate. The MCC

came in for some sharp criticism and were compelled to forward an explanation.'

There was also a curious controversy with the touring team over the hours of play in matches other than Tests. The Australians insisted that in their match against MCC the hours of play should be 12 to 6, although the game had been advertised to continue until 6.30, when it was stated that stumps would be drawn. It seems a very odd issue to have provoked a dispute.

Middlesex were captained that year by F.T. Mann, who was to share with the Cowdreys a remarkable record. Both F.T. Mann and his son George in their time captained

Middlesex County Cricket Club, 1922.

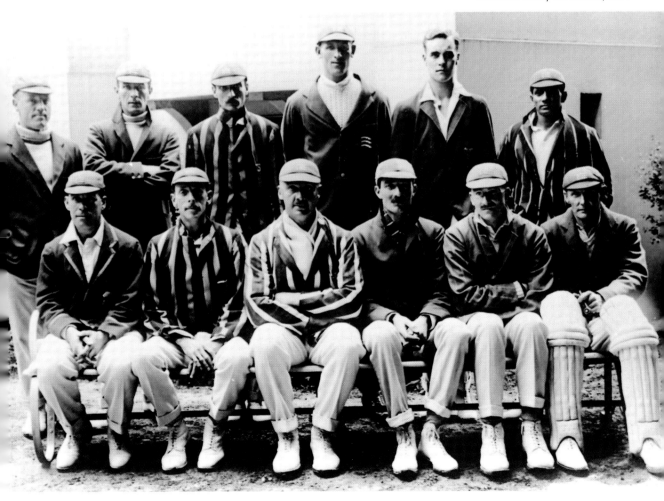

England. Under the captaincy of F.T. Mann, Middlesex won the county championship for the second year in succession. In University cricket Gilbert, Hubert and Claude Ashton (all of Winchester and Trinity) captained the light blues successively in 1921 and the two subsequent years. They equalled the record of the fellow Trinity College cricketers, G.B., C.T. and J.E.K. Studd. These Etonians captained Cambridge in successive years from 1882 to 1884. In 1923 Oxford won in two days by an innings and 227 runs. This was the most decisive margin in the whole of this historic series.

In 1925 Percy Holmes scored 315 not out when he played for Yorkshire against Middlesex. This beat the previous record score at Lord's which William Ward had made over 100 years previously. Holmes was not destined to hold on to his record for long, however. In the very next season, 1926, Jack Hobbs made 316 not out when he

appeared for Surrey in their local derby against Middlesex. This remained the record score for the headquarters of cricket until Graham Gooch came to beat it when he made his historic innings of 333 for England against India in 1990.

In 1926 Francis Lacey ended the longest tenure in office of any MCC Secretary. After 28 years in his post, he retired in that year and was succeeded by William Findlay. Lacey was deservedly honoured with a knighthood, thereby becoming, as we have already seen, the first person to receive that high distinction for his services to the game. Lord's and MCC clearly owed him an incalculable debt. If one can draw some conclusions from his portrait by G. Spencer Watson which hangs in the Committee Room, they are that he may not have suffered fools gladly, but he certainly served the club, the ground and the game in general with great distinction and high devotion.

six

1926 – 1946

PEACE AND WAR

HENRY
JOHNS
· Lord's ·
1937-1975

ANTHONY HOBSON

Henry Johns, the head tennis professional at Lord's for many
years, as painted by Antony Hobson in 1975.

As everyone imagined would be the case, Sir Francis Lacey proved to be a very hard act to follow. He had, however, a very worthy and competent successor in Billy Findlay who took over as Secretary of MCC in 1926. He had previously turned out for Eton, Oxford University and Lancashire.

The New Zealanders came on their first cricket tour of England in 1927 under the captaincy of T.C. Lowry. They played twice at Lord's – in matches against Middlesex and MCC. King George V came to watch part of the first day of the county game. Also that year the centenary of the Oxford and Cambridge match was celebrated. Lord Harris was in the chair – there could be nobody who would have been more appropriate. As Lord Harris himself remarked, he had known at least one player in every match since the first one in 1827.

The England XI, 1926

The MCC touring party to South America, 1926, which featured Alec Douglas-Home, the future Prime Minister and President of MCC (on the ground, right).

King George V at Lord's, *c*. 1926.

The West Indians were granted Test match status in 1928. They were beaten by an innings at Lord's, but their fast bowling was formidable. Herbert Sutcliffe told Pelham Warner during the Lord's Test that he had never played finer pace bowling. Learie Constantine was their star player – his fielding was as brilliant as his bowling. His one Achilles heel was that he failed as a batsman in the Tests. 1928 also witnessed a very exciting University match; Oxford achieved a splendid rearguard action to force a draw. In the same week Eton beat Harrow by 28 runs in a fine game 15 minutes before time.

In the following September MCC sent a team to Australia under the captaincy of Percy Chapman. The batting was so strong that Frank Woolley was omitted. Those were the days! The great left-handers, Phil Mead and Maurice Leyland, only played in one Test match apiece. England was victorious by four matches to one. The Manager, Mr F.C. Toone of Yorkshire CCC, was knighted on his return but, alas, he died soon afterwards.

One of the young amateurs whom Findlay will undoubtedly have encountered in his early days as Secretary was a Middlesex cricketer who had the resounding name of George Oswald Browning Allen but who was almost universally known as 'Gubby'. This Old Etonian cricket blue from Cambridge became very much the *éminence grise* at Lord's during the latter part of the twentieth century. In 1929, when he was playing for Middlesex against Lancashire, Gubby had what in all probability he regarded as his finest hour, taking all ten wickets in an innings. This is the only time in history that this remarkable feat has ever been performed at Lord's in a county championship match. Gubby Allen was perhaps the finest player never to have been nominated by *Wisden Cricketers' Almanack* as one of its Five Cricketers of the Year. His considerable business interests prevented him from playing cricket with any great regularity. As we shall shortly see, he was an important member of the famous MCC team which toured Australia under the captaincy of Douglas Jardine in 1932/33.

There were 5,724 MCC members in 1930. That year was probably most notable in the history of the game for witnessing the first appearance in this country of a young Australian batsman named Don Bradman. The youthful cricketing genius made an indelible impression at Lord's. He celebrated his first Test match at the home of cricket by scoring an ever-memorable 254 in one of the greatest games of all time.

History was also made the following year by a last-minute replacement for Cambridge in the Varsity Match, when a T. Ratcliffe for the light blues hammered the Oxford attack, amassing a total of 201. This record score for the historic series, however, only lasted for less than 24 hours. The very next day the elder Nawab of Pataudi had his revenge for the dark blues and made a score of 238 not

G.O.B. (Sir George) Allen by John Ward, RA.

Lord Harris by Arthur Hacker.

out for Oxford. This is still a record in the matches between our oldest universities. The following season of 1932 witnessed the first Test match played by India at the headquarters of cricket.

The previous year had seen the eightieth birthday of Lord Harris, who in his time served India well as Governor of Bombay and who had become the great elder statesman of the game. His words on becoming an octogenarian are justly famous:

'Cricket has been too good a friend to me for nearly seventy years for me to part with it one moment before I have to. I cannot remember a time when it did not convey its friendly welcome… I have been fairly busy for most of my life, but never so busy that the thought of cricket and my companions were not an inspiration to get on with the work that I might enjoy its invigorating capacity… And in my message to youth I will repeat what I said to the half-holiday cricketer. You do well to love it, for it is freer from anything sordid, anything dishonourable, than any game in the world. To play it keenly, honourably, generously, self-sacrificingly, is a moral lesson in itself and the classroom is God's air and sunshine. Foster it, my brothers, so that it may attract all who can find the time to play it, protect it from anything that would sully it so that it may grow in favour with all men.'

Lord Harris died a year later at the ripe old age of eighty-one. It is a pity that his noble sentiments were not more to the forefront when MCC toured Australia a few months after his passing. The 'bodyline' tour of 1932/33, as it came to be known, was the most contentious cricketing issue in the period between the wars. It is alleged that the old housemaster of Douglas Jardine, the MCC captain, was asked in 1932 what he thought would be England's chances in the forthcoming Ashes series. The old Winchester College master thought for a moment and then he is reputed to have replied that he was sure that England would win the Ashes under the captaincy of Jardine, but that there would also be a grave risk that a great dominion might be lost in the process.

The housemaster was not so very wide of the mark. The exchanges, which were made between MCC and the authorities back in Australia, do not make for very edifying reading, to put it at its mildest. The weighty issues which were raised by bodyline tactics are reliably believed to have been discussed at Cabinet level in both the respective countries. It was a truly melancholy episode in the history

Lord Harris as drawn by Spy.

The MCC team in Australia, 1932/33.

of the game. One notable exception to this stricture was Gubby Allen, who steadfastly refused to take part in what he regarded as being unfair tactics. One important potential peacemaker was Sir Alexander Hore Ruthven VC (who later became Lord Gowrie). He was the Governor of South Australia at the time and he did his level best to heal an ugly situation. His private secretary, Mr C. Leigh Winser, was a cricketer and much later, in 1971, he presented to the MCC Library the fascinating correspondence which went to and from Government House, Adelaide at this sensitive time.

Both during and also after the tour a veritable barrage of cables passed between Lord's and the Australian Board of Control. The exchange started on 18 January 1933 when this blunt missive was received by MCC:

'Bodyline bowling has assumed such proportions as to menace the best interests of the game, making protection of the body by the batsmen the main consideration.

'This is causing intensely bitter feelings between the players as well as injury. In our opinion it is unsportsmanlike.'

The use of the word 'unsportsmanlike' stung just where it hurt. Five days later MCC cabled back:

'We, Marylebone Cricket Club, deplore your cable. We deprecate your opinion that there has been unsportsmanlike play. We have the fullest confidence in captain, team and managers and are convinced that they would do nothing to infringe either the laws of cricket or the spirit of the game…

'We hope the situation is not so serious as your cable would seem to indicate, but if it is such as to jeopardise the good relations between English and Australian cricketers and you consider it desirable to cancel remainder of programme, we would consent, but with great reluctance.'

The Australian Board sent their reply on the following 30 January:

'We appreciate your difficulty in dealing with the matter raised in our cable without having seen the actual play. We unanimously regard bodyline bowling, as adopted in some of the games in the present tour, as opposed to the spirit of cricket, and unnecessarily dangerous to the players.

'We are deeply concerned that the ideals of the game should be protected and have therefore appointed a committee to report on the action necessary to eliminate such bowling from Australian cricket as from the beginning of the 1933/34 season. We do not consider it necessary to cancel remainder of programme.'

The MCC Committee were doubtless very relieved to have this message and on 2 February they cabled back:

'We note with pleasure that you do not consider it necessary to cancel remainder of programme… May we accept this as a clear indication that the good sportsmanship of our team is not in question?

'When your recommendation reaches us it shall receive our most careful consideration and will be submitted to the Imperial Cricket Conference.'

The Australian Board made a conciliatory reply on 8 February:

'We do not regard the sportsmanship of your team as being in question.

'We join heartily with you in hoping the remaining Tests will be played with the traditional good feeling.'

England touring cap from the 1930s, featuring St George slaying the dragon.

There was an important meeting of the Australian Board on 21 April 1933. As a result of the deliberations taken on that occasion, a further cable was sent to MCC with the suggestion that the following should be added to the Laws of Cricket.

'Any ball delivered which, in the opinion of the umpire at the bowler's end is bowled at the batsman to intimidate or injure him shall be considered unfair and "No-ball" shall be called.'

A reply was forthcoming from MCC on 12 June:

'The new Law recommended by the Australian Board of Control does not appear to the Committee to be practicable. Firstly it would place an impossible task on the umpire and secondly, it would place in the hands of the umpire a power over the game which would be more than dangerous and which any umpire might well fear to exercise.'

Attention was also drawn in the MCC reply to:

'Barracking…against which there is unanimous depreciation. Barracking has, unfortunately, always been indulged in by spectators from Australia to a degree quite unknown in this country. During the late tour, however, it would appear to have exceeded all previous experience and on occasions to have been thoroughly objectionable.'

The Australian reply was sent on 22 September:

'We are giving consideration to the question of barracking and you will rely upon our using our best endeavours to have it controlled on future tours.

'We are most anxious that the cordial relations which have so long existed between English and Australian cricket shall continue.'

MCC's reply on 5 October was in a similarly tactful vein:

'Your team can certainly take the field with the knowledge and with full assurance that cricket will be played here in the same spirit as in the past and with the single desire to promote the best interests of the game in both countries.

'Your team can rely on a warm welcome from MCC and every effort will be made to make their visit enjoyable.'

A meeting was held at Lord's on 23 November 1933 which decided that no change in the laws of the game was desirable, but that any form of bowling which was a direct attack by the bowler upon the batsman would be an offence against the spirit of cricket. It was decided to leave the latter to the captains in the complete confidence that they would not permit or even countenance bowling of such type.

The final exchanges in the long saga were as follows. MCC cabled the Australian Board:

'We shall welcome Australian cricketers who come to play cricket with us next year. If, however, your Board of Control decide that such games should be deferred we shall regret their decision.

'Please let us know your Board's final decision as soon as possible and in any event before the end of the year.'

On 14 December the Australians replied:

'With reference to your cable of October 9 and your confirmatory cable of December 12 in reply to ours of November 16, we too now regard the position finalised. Our team will leave Australia on March 9.'

The final reply from MCC was sent on 14 December:

'Thank you for your cable. We are glad to know we may look forward to welcoming the Australians next summer. We shall do all in our power to make their visit enjoyable.'

Cricket's greatest contest was thus saved for posterity but had been, as they say, a 'close run thing'. A less contentious note was sounded in 1934 with the laying out of an attractive garden in memory of Lord Harris. This was approached through a gate that was designed by Sir Herbert Baker. Lord Harris, as we have seen, was a veteran of Fitzgerald's tour to North America back in 1872, which had incurred the wrath of Mr Gladstone's government. He succeeded Dr W.G. Grace as the Grand Old Man of English cricket. He was President of MCC in Grace's *annus mirabilis* of 1895 and he was Treasurer of the club from 1916 (when he succeeded Sir Spencer Ponsonby-Fane) until his death in 1932. The Harris Garden is the venue where countless team photographs have been taken. Its roses have thus become famous.

Q Stand was also opened in 1934. This too was designed by Sir Herbert Baker and indeed it was the last structure at Lord's to have been erected by that great architect. It was subsequently renamed the Allen Stand in honour of Sir George who in his turn took on the mantle of the club's *éminence grise*. Another embellishment for Lord's came with the presentation of a sculpture by Gilbert Bayes RA. The donor was Alderman David Isaacs. The sculpture is situated at the busy junction of the Wellington and St John's Wood Roads. Its surrounds have recently been landscaped and it now looks as good as new. It bears the famous legend 'Play up, play up and play the game'.

Right top and bottom: Gargoyles on the pavilion of Sir Spencer Ponsonby-Fane (top) and Lord Harris.

Below: W. Findlay as a player.

The first South African side to defeat England at Lord's, 1935.

It was very fortunate that Anglo/Australian cricketing links were maintained in 1934 because that year saw England's only victory over Australia at Lord's in the whole of the twentieth century. Indeed, it was the only time that England has defeated the old enemy at the headquarters of cricket since 1896. The hero of the match was Hedley Verity, who took 14 Australian wickets in a day. He was killed in action ten years later – this was, perhaps, the greatest cricketing loss of the Second World War.

In 1936 Billy Findlay retired and made way for Colonel R.S. Rait Kerr to assume the mantle of Secretary of MCC. Findlay was, so to speak, 'sandwiched' between two outstanding administrators of great ability and influence, but he himself was a remarkable man in his own right. It is noteworthy that no less a person than Field Marshal Lord Plumer said of him, 'If Findlay had been a soldier I should have liked to have had him on my staff'. Colonel Rait Kerr (or R.K. as he was generally known) combined his remarkable executive skills with a profound knowledge of the history and the interpretation of the laws of cricket. This was a subject in which he was a great expert. Sir Pelham Warner paid him the ultimate compliment: 'It is no disparagement to former holders of the office to say that Rait Kerr is the ablest Secretary the MCC has ever pos-

sessed.' R.K. saw Lord's safely through a very difficult time of war and peace with much efficiency. As we shall also see, he was not the only able member of his family to serve Lord's with distinction.

On a humbler note Lord's witnessed an odd incident on 3 July 1936. Jehangir Khan was bowling to T.N. Pearce when the ball killed a sparrow. This took place during the Cambridge University *v* MCC match. The sparrow was eventually sent to a taxidermist and is now a popular exhibit in the MCC Museum.

During the following year of 1937 the country witnessed the Coronation of King George VI and Queen Elizabeth. It was an equally important year for Lord's with the celebration of the club's 150th anniversary. Colonel the Hon. J.J. Astor was President of MCC that year and he arranged for *The Times* to honour the occasion with the publication of a special commemorative book. It is a delightful period piece. In the introduction, under the heading 'An Imperial Institution' we read '…the MCC will not be hustled in spite of the modern demand for speed and excitement'.

Colonel Astor takes up the same theme:

'This volume tells in particular the story of the MCC and Lord's and generally reviews the past and present of cricket throughout the Empire. So true has the game proved to the taste and character of generations of the English race that it continues to thrive in spite of modern haste and competition of rival pastimes. The white figures of its players against the trees of summer still form one of the fairest and most home-like of English scenes. On our school playing fields, our village greens and on impromptu pitches, where unhappily there are not better, it is the initiation of our youth into manliness…'

On a sadder note, 1937 saw the retirement of one of Lord's most memorable and charismatic figures, the much loved 'Patsy' Hendren. Cricketers mainly remember the following season for Len Hutton's majestic and record-breaking 364, which he amassed at The Oval, but the Lord's Test of that year was also noteworthy in its own way.

Walter Hammond made a great score of 240 in that match. In addition the shape of things to come was signified by the introduction of television cameras at the ground. The Lord's Test of 1938 has been immortalised for cricketing art lovers because Charles Cundall, RA painted a famous panoramic view of the ground during that match. Almost all the buildings which one can see in the painting, except for the cluster around the pavilion, have since been demolished or (as in the case of the Mound Stand) have been modernised almost out of all recognition. The old St John's Wood power station is prominently shown in Mr Cundall's work. Few mourned when that building was taken down after the last war. Mr Cundall served in that conflict with great distinction as a war artist.

On a sadder note Martin Bladen, Seventh Baron Hawke died on 19 October 1938. He was, unusually for those days, a Yorkshire cricketer who had not been born in the county. He was especially connected with the game in the white rose county, but he was also a very influential person at Lord's. He was President of MCC throughout the period of the First World War and he succeeded Lord Harris as Treasurer of the club in 1932.

In the off-season of 1938/39 MCC took a team to South Africa under the captaincy of Walter Hammond. It is perhaps most memorable for the 'Timeless Test' which had to end as a draw after ten days so that the players could catch the boat back home.

The last pre-war season of 1939 witnessed the tour of the West Indian team. The young hopefuls Len Hutton and Denis Compton both made centuries in the Lord's Test. They added 246 for the fourth wicket in only 140 minutes but the great star of the match was George Headley, who became the first cricketer to score a century in each innings in a Test match at Lord's.

On the outbreak of hostilities in 1939 Colonel Rait Kerr and his deputy, Mr Ronald Aird (the Assistant Secretary) were soon mobilised into the army. Both men were to be decorated for their gallant and distinguished services. Colonel Rait Kerr was awarded the CBE for his work with War Office Selection Boards whilst Mr Aird won the Military Cross.

The elderly Sir Pelham Warner held the fort at Lord's as Acting Secretary with great devotion and unselfishness. The Royal Air Force occupied large portions of the ground by the end of June 1941. The main use to which the RAF put Lord's was as an Air Crew Reception area. As the name implies many young men had their first taste of service life when they reported to Lord's. Recently a commemorative plaque has been placed on the pavilion outer wall recording the contribution the ground made to the winning of the war.

Below: MCC members at a dinner, to celebrate MCC's 150th anniversary, 1937.

Bottom: MCC team in South Africa, 1938/39. This was the last pre-war touring team.

England *v.* Australia at Lord's, 1938, by Charles Cundall RA (1890-1971).

Lord's precious artefacts were put into storage during the war.

The Committee Room in wartime.

There was fortunately much more cricket being played at Lord's during this conflict compared with the similar situation in the First World War. Public attitudes (unlike the situation which prevailed in 1914) did not regard it as unpatriotic to play and indeed the powers that be thought that the game would be a good morale booster. One prisoner of war received a message during his captivity, which told him that he had been 'elected to Lord's', whereupon he was treated with more deference by his captors who were under the misapprehension that he had been ennobled!

The most celebrated wartime incident at Lord's happened on 29 July 1944 when a flying bomb flew over the ground and began to cut out. After an enforced and very noisy interval Captain Jack Robertson resumed his position at the crease and very nonchalantly hit the second

Above and below: Lord's during the Second World War.

Barrage balloon at Lord's.

ball, which he received for six. Some of the intrepid players and spectators who attended Lord's for that noted match have formed the Buzz Bomb Club and they hold reunions from time to time at the ground.

The closest shave which Lord's experienced during the war, however, took place on the night of 17/18 January 1943, when an unexploded 500 kilogram bomb was found by Major W.G. Parker. It had penetrated the Bakerloo Line – which in those days used to run under the Nursery Ground. Captain F. Carlyle, demonstrating the utmost gallantry, had it removed from the ground to Hampstead Heath, where he secured it. When he examined the fuse,

Captain Carlyle found it to be longer than any previous German example.

When peace came, MCC elected the great war leaders to Honorary Life Membership of the club. Those honoured were Field Marshal Viscount Alexander of Tunis, the Right Honourable Winston S. Churchill, Admiral of the Fleet Viscount Cunningham of Hyndhope, Admiral of the Fleet Lord Fraser of Northcape, Admiral of the Fleet Earl Mountbatten of Burma, Field Marshal Viscount Alanbrooke of Brookeborough, Field Marshal Viscount Montgomery of Alamein, Marshal of the RAF Viscount Portal of Hungerford and Marshal of the RAF Lord

Tedder of Glenguin. General of the US Army Dwight D. Eisenhower was similarly honoured, but it seems unlikely that he ever visited Lord's.

Lord's could now breathe a sigh of relief and the club could consider itself to have been very lucky indeed. The synagogue opposite had received a direct hit and the Sabbath services were held from time to time in the pavilion. The only casualty of any significance at Lord's was a very well-known one. Father Time was 'yorked' by the cable of a barrage balloon. He slid gently on to the balcony seats before he could be rescued. He spent the remaining years of the war in the august surroundings of the Committee Room. When peace came he was restored to his original perch and he stayed for many years on top of Sir Herbert Baker's grandstand. His equilibrium was again disturbed when he was damaged in the great storm of October 1987. More recently he had had to be moved to

RAAF presentation to MCC.

RAF *v.* The Rest scorecard, 1941.
Note the instructions concerning air raids.

A unique photograph of the moment when a flying bomb disrupted a wartime match.

Field Marshal Montgomery pictured at Lord's in 1944.

the opposite side of the ground when the new grandstand was erected.

Three Victory Tests took place on the ground in 1945, whilst a match between England and the Dominions attracted no fewer than 90,000 spectators. The game was made ever memorable by the splendid batting of Wally Hammond together with that of the young Australian Keith Miller and of the New Zealander Martin Donnelly.

Colonel Rait Kerr and Major Aird returned to Lord's from their distinguished wartime service in the army. When they had resumed their peacetime duties, they recruited the Colonel's daughter, Diana, as a 'temporary

measure'. Diana Rait Kerr also had a gallant war record – in her case driving ambulances during the Blitz. She now had the formidable task of sorting out MCC's many and varied literary and artistic treasures. They had been evacuated for the duration of the war to Stoke Hammond Rectory. Fortunately for all concerned, the 'temporary' stay continued for 23 years until she finally retired in 1968.

Lord's welcomed an Indian touring team in 1946 and life at the ground began to return to some degree of normality. The following season, however, to the delight of cricketers everywhere proved to be far from normal.

seven

1946 – 1963

THE POST-WAR SCENE

Denis Compton.

The Club entered the post-war period with 7,174 members – 1,450 more than in 1930. They were able to witness in 1947 one of the great English cricket seasons. The golden summer which shone on England was just the tonic that the country and the game in general sorely needed. The previous winter had seen some grim and bitter weather – in addition, post-war austerity was everywhere in evidence. The poor performance of the MCC team in Australia in 1946/47 had done but little to lift the spirits of followers of the game, although in fairness MCC only sent a team down under in response to popular demand in both countries. From the point of view of England's chances it would have been much better to have had considerably longer in which to recover from the great hiatus caused by the Second World War.

All this doom and gloom, however, was to vanish during the 1947 season. The 'terrible twins' consisting of Denis Compton and Bill Edrich were to delight the great crowds throughout the country in a glorious summer with their positive orgy of run getting. Denis Compton made no fewer than 18 centuries in the process of amassing a record 3,816 runs that season at an average of 90.85. Bill Edrich, fresh from his gallant wartime exploits, which earned for him the Distinguished Flying Cross, also broke all previous records with his total of 3,539 runs at an average of 80.43. These colossal aggregates have never been exceeded in subsequent seasons. To cap it all, Middlesex sped to their first championship win since the triumphant swan song of Plum Warner back in 1921.

In the following season of 1948 the great pair put on an unbroken third wicket at partnership of 424 for Middlesex in their match against Somerset at Lord's. This was, almost incredibly, achieved in just four scintillating hours. On the whole, however, the season proved to be a very disappointing

Compton and Edrich walk out to bat, 1947.

The future Secretary of MCC, S.C. Griffith, keeps wicket as Donald Bradman bats.

Sir Donald Bradman, 1972, by R. Hannaford.

time at the headquarters of cricket. This was due not least to England's almost total failure to mount an effective counter-attack against Don Bradman's all-conquering Australian team. The tourists who came to England in the 1948 season can put up a very good claim to have constituted the most formidable cricketing force that the world has ever seen.

Don Bradman's fortieth birthday coincided with his farewell appearance at Lord's in the match against the Gentlemen of England. He made a mere 150 in this game. In honour of the occasion George Portman created a tremendous birthday cake. Mr Portman was the famous caterer at Lord's and was on the verge of his own retirement after 50 years with MCC. An even more legendary figure was commemorated during the Gentlemen v. Players match. The game very nearly coincided with the

centenary of the birth of W.G. Grace and a handsome wreath was placed on the Grace Gates.

Immediately after Christmas an MCC team departed for the West Indies under the captaincy of Gubby Allen who was indeed elderly if judged by modern standards. It was not a very representative team and it was dogged by injury. The team failed to win a single one of their 11 matches although they only actually lost twice.

The New Zealanders were the tourists in 1949 and Middlesex were joint county champions with Yorkshire. The year was particularly notable because it was then that the Duke of Edinburgh honoured MCC by becoming the President for the first time. The club granted honorary cricket membership to 26 retired professional players of great distinction. They were S.F. Barnes, C.J. Barnett,

The King and Queen visit Lord's in 1948.

The Long Room photographed in 1946.

The Long Room by Hanslip Fletcher, 1949.

C.B. Fry (1872-1956), *c.* 1950, by Edmund Nelson.
Mr Nelson was the brother-in-law of E.W. Swanton.

L.C. Braund, G. Duckworth, A.P. Freeman, G. Geary, G. Gunn Senior, J.W. Hearne, E. Hendren, G.H. Hirst, J.B. Hobbs, H. Larwood, M. Leyland, C.P. Mead, E. Paynter, W. Rhodes, A.C. Russell, A. Sandham, E.J. Smith, H. Strudwick, H. Sutcliffe, M.W. Tate, E. Tyldesley, W. Voce and F.E. Woolley. They were indeed great names to conjure with.

On 20 April 1949 Jimmy Cannon died. He started working at Lord's in the tennis courts as far back as 1879. In his early days he used to hold the horses' heads for members. He served for 65 years at Lord's and finished his career as Chief Clerk – more importantly, he was the folk memory of MCC.

1950 was particularly noteworthy in the annals of the game on account of the victory calypso that greeted the success of the West Indies in the Lord's Test Match. It is doubtful whether cricket's headquarters had ever before heard anything like this.

> *Cricket, lovely cricket*
> *At Lord's where I saw it*
> *Cricket, lovely cricket*
> *At Lord's where I saw it*
> *Yardley tried his best*
> *But Goddard won the Test*
> *They gave the crowd plenty of fun*
> *Second Test and West Indians won*

> Chorus
> *With those two little pals of mine*
> *Ramadhin and Valentine*

Several verses later the calypso ends:
> *West Indies were feeling homely*
> *Their audience had them happy*
> *When Washbrook's century had ended*
> *West Indies voices all blended*
> *Hats went in the air*
> *They jumped and shouted without fear*

> *So at Lord's was the scenery*
> *Bound to go down in history*

> Chorus
> *After all was said and done*
> *Second Test and West Indies won!*

1950 was also noteworthy because in that year the Grand Old Man of Lord's, Sir Pelham Warner, assumed the Presidency. Mr William Findlay, the former Secretary of MCC, succeeded him the following year, which saw the visit of the South African touring team. To everyone's surprise Oxford beat the Cambridge team which included cricketers of the calibre of Messrs Sheppard, May, Subba Row, Warr and Wait.

The Duke of Edinburgh and Sir Robert Menzies at Lord's.

Sir Pelham Warner by Katharine Lloyd.

The Indians were the tourists in 1952 whilst in the field of administration Colonel Rait Kerr retired to be succeeded by his long service deputy, Mr Ronald Aird. It was a great pity that the Second World War cut R.K.'s period of office in two. He was such an able administrator that it is interesting to speculate what he might have accomplished in an uninterrupted incumbency unencumbered by post-war restrictions and austerities.

The following season of 1953 coincided with the Coronation of HM Queen Elizabeth II and with the conquest of Mount Everest. It was therefore entirely in accordance with the spirit of things that HRH Prince Philip, Duke of Edinburgh, should have been the one to open what was then rather grandiloquently known as The Imperial Cricket Memorial Gallery. In more recent years this anachronistic mouthful has been altered to the MCC Museum. The Gallery was converted from the old racquets court to the designs of Mr J.H. Markham.

It was intended to be a war memorial and it was dedicated as such by the Rt Revd and Rt Hon. William Wand, the Bishop of London. It commemorates cricketers of all lands who have given their lives in the cause of freedom.

The memorial tablet is made of the beautiful Hopton Wood stone from Derbyshire. In fine lettering it bears these noble words which were originally penned by the American poet, J.R. Lowell, 'Secure from change in their high-hearted ways'. The Hon. George Lyttleton, who served for many years on the MCC Arts and Library Sub-Committee and who was a member of the famous cricketing family, selected these moving words.

Top right: The Duke of Edinburgh opens what is now known as the MCC Museum, 1953.
Bottom left: The old raquets court, which was converted into the MCC Museum.
Bottom right: Colonel R.S. Rait Kerr (1891-1961), drawn in 1966 by John Stanton Ward.

The Long Room at Lord's, 1953, by Dennis Flanders.

Diana Rait Kerr, First Curator of the MCC 1945-1968, 1978, by John Ward.

The Lord's scoreboard assists in the celebrations for Sir Pelham Warner's birthday.

The club has had a collection of artistic and historical treasures since the 1860s when MCC acquired some paintings when it took over the ground from Mr J.H. Dark. The MCC Museum has indeed some considerable claim to be one of the oldest established sporting museums in the world. For many years in the inter-war period Captain T.H. Carlton Levick looked after this side of MCC's activities. This he did with great devotion and in an honorary capacity. He did, however, often spend the

English winter accompanying MCC touring teams and it was only really with the appointment of Diana Rait Kerr in a full-time capacity in 1945 that substantial genuine progress could be made. Until 1953 most of the collection was housed in the pavilion at Lord's. This was doubly unsatisfactory – not only were conditions there not really up to acceptable modern standards but on non-match days it was very difficult for the fair sex or for men who were non-members or for children to gain access to the collection. The creation of a gallery in 1953 which was open to the general public relieved the pressure of space in the pavilion and enabled the collection to become much more accessible and attractively displayed. For twenty-three years Diana Rait Kerr was Curator of MCC. She was an acknowledged expert on many facets of the game's literary and artistic heritage, not least in the whole area of the evolution of the dress worn by cricketers.

1953 was indeed a great year. The cricketing climax came with the winning of the Ashes under the leadership of Len Hutton, England's first professional captain. Its emotional climax probably came in the autumn when Sir Pelham's eightieth birthday was celebrated with a great dinner in his honour in the Long Room. The Grandstand scoreboard was floodlit and read '80 NOT OUT'.

Queen Elizabeth II greets the Australian team, 1953.

The visiting Pakistani team, 1954.

1954 was a very wet summer. MCC was very glad to welcome for the first time to Lord's a visiting Pakistani touring team. The next season, by contrast, was dry and sunny and witnessed the arrival of the South African tourists. In the intervening off-season Len Hutton's team had regained the Ashes in Australia. 1955 marked the bicentenary of Thomas Lord. On 24 July the President of MCC, Lord Cobham, who was a member of the famous Lyttleton family, presented to the cricketers of Thirsk a carved oak plaque. The following month an MCC team went with cricketers from West Meon and Warnford from the cricket ground to the founder's tomb to pay their respects. They then downed a pint (or two) at the recently renamed Thomas Lord Inn.

Thomas Lord's tombstone, 1951.

England continued its winning sequence against Australia in 1956, although the most sensational game that year was not at Lord's but at Old Trafford where Jim Laker took his incredible 19 wickets. In 1957 Cambridge defeated their dark blue opponents by an innings and 186 runs. This was the highest margin in the annals of this most historic of Lord's fixtures. The Varsity matches at this time still had the power to attract very substantial crowds.

Sir Pelham opened the Warner Stand in 1958 – its architect was Mr Kenneth Peacock. It was built on the site of the old 'A' Enclosure. 1959 was as sunny as 1958 had been wet. India were beaten in three days in the Lord's Test. The following year the Test against South Africa proved to be a very frustrating one for M.J.K. Smith. If he had been able to score but one single more run he would have joined the select band that consists of Percy Chapman and Martin Donnelly. They alone have the distinction of having made hundreds at Lord's in the University Match, in a Test and in the Gentlemen v. Players fixture. The occasion was even sadder for the South African bowler, George Griffin. Earlier in the game he had performed the hat-trick but in the exhibition match that followed England's victory, Griffin was repeatedly no-balled for throwing and his career ended prematurely.

The Australians were the touring side in 1961. They retained the Ashes, which they had won in 1958/59. The Oxford v. Cambridge match was marred by the absence of the captain of the dark blues, the Nawab of Pataudi. He had been seriously injured in a car accident in Brighton shortly beforehand.

The Long Room in 1956.

Ronald Aird, drawn in 1964 by John Ward.

The Pakistani touring team of 1962 were again unlucky with the weather. The year was particularly notable for the retirement of Mr Ronald Aird. He had served MCC with great loyalty and distinction for 36 years. He was succeeded by Mr S.C. Griffith who was almost universally known to members and to cricketers as Billy or the Colonel. The latter sobriquet was a reference to his gallant wartime service in the Glider Pilot Regiment for which he was awarded the Distinguished Flying Cross. The former name came about because it was believed that his parents wanted to call their son William Cathie Griffith but that they realised in the nick of time that the initials 'WC' might well prove in later life to be somewhat of a liability. Billy Griffith performed the remarkable feat of scoring his maiden century in first-class cricket on his Test debut. This was in the Test match between England and the West Indies on the 1947/48 MCC tour.

1962 was also a year that has gone down in the history of the game because it was during that season that the last Gentlemen *v.* Players match was staged. A series that had its origins on the original Lord's ground in 1806 was to end when amateur status was abolished in the first-class game. This was an inevitable move although not a few missed the more carefree approach to the game which many amateurs were able to contribute to cricket.

Sir Pelham Warner, who was to die in 1963, had written one of the standard histories of this historic fixture. His father had been born two days before the Battle of Trafalgar took place, yet Sir Pelham was to live until the year in which the Gillette Cup was inaugurated. This was the first knockout championship in top class cricket. Moreover its introduction into the fixture list was a further sign of the willingness of MCC to move with the times. Not all the county cricket clubs had by any means been keen on the idea originally. The annual fixture at the end of the summer became a grand curtain call on the season. The large and excited crowds contributed to a Wembley-like atmosphere.

1963 was also noteworthy because one of the very greatest Test matches of all time took place at Lord's that year. It happened when England played the West Indies. Wes Hall bowled superlatively well and when he started the last over of the match no fewer than four results were still possible. A run-out off the fourth ball brought the injured Colin Cowdrey, his arm in plaster, to the non-striker's end. With nine wickets down David Allen did not dare risk exposing his handicapped partner and England finished only six very tantalising runs short of their target. In the entire history of the game there have been witnessed few more exciting draws. An indication of the way the game gripped the imagination of the whole country lay in the fact that even the BBC television news had to wait – it started late to enable the vast watching public to see the gripping conclusion to this epic match.

S.C. Griffith, pictured in 1974 by John Ward.

Sir Pelham Warner at the official opening of the Warner Stand in 1958.

eight

1963 – 1987

CONSOLIDATION AND CONTROVERSY

A sketch of the Old Tavern, demolished in the 1960s to make way for the
Tavern Stand.

The year 1964 witnessed double celebrations. It was the year of the 150th anniversary of the present Lord's Ground and it marked the centenary of Middlesex County Cricket Club. To honour the former event, Lord Cobham used his influence as President of the Worcestershire County Cricket Club and as the county's Lord Lieutenant to see that MCC received a beautiful accession. The Royal Worcester Company kindly presented to the club a lovely bowl to mark 150 years on the present ground. In those days the tourists used to start their season with the traditional match on the picturesque ground at Worcester. The Royal Worcester Company used to produce a limited edition of plates bearing the signatures of the latest touring team.

Late in 1964 Lord's suffered a sad bereavement. *Wisden* for 1965 carried an unusual obituary which read:

'CAT, PETER, whose ninth life ended on 5 November 1964, was a well-known cricket watcher at Lord's where he spent 12 of his 14 years. He preferred a close-up view of the proceedings and his sleek, black form could often be seen prowling on the field of play when the crowds were biggest. He frequently appeared on the television screen. Mr S.C. Griffith, Secretary of M.C.C., said of him – "He was a cat of great character and loved publicity."'

One of Peter's successors bore the apt name of Oval.

In 1965 two major tourists came to Lord's for the first double of its kind. The immense popularity of the 1963 West Indies tourists had led to demands that they should be seen again in this country before too long had elapsed. Double tours were deemed to be the answer. The West Indians returned in 1966 but their four matches at Lord's were all drawn.

In some ways the 150th anniversary celebrations marked the end of an era. The old and much loved Tavern was to be demolished – this venerable building had almost reached its own century having been erected in 1868. It was, however, a difficult place to manage and in its stead a public house and banqueting suite facing St John's Wood Road joined the amenities of Lord's. What might be said to have been lost in atmosphere had been gained in increased efficiency and capacity.

In 1966 the former Prime Minister, Sir Alec Douglas Home became President of MCC. He was the only Premier to have played first-class cricket and, as Lord Dunglass, he had toured South America with the MCC team in 1926/27. He made the memorable jocular remark that he had had to handle more paperwork as President of MCC than when he was Prime Minister.

Royal Worcester Bowl, to celebrate 150 years at the present Lord's, 1814-1964.

Construction work at Lord's in the 1960s.

The construction of the Tavern Stand, 1967.

The crowd in the newly finished Tavern Stand enjoying a Test match.

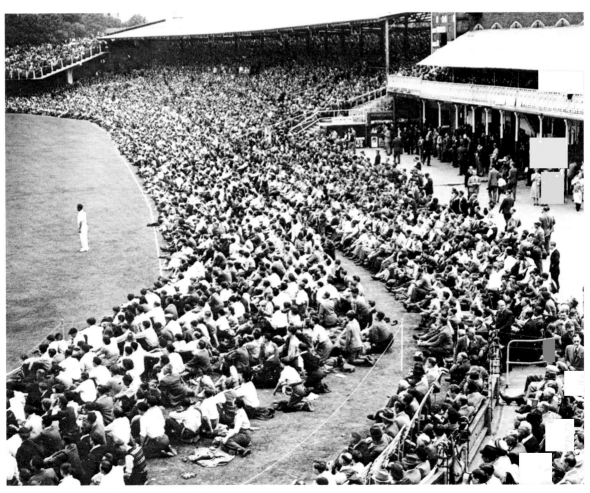

The 1948 Test as seen from the old Tavern Stand.

1967 was a wet year and the Indian tourists had the worst of the weather. The Pakistani team were a little more fortunate with their experiences of the vagaries of the English climate. The Australians toured England in 1968 and the year was also memorable for the erection of the Tavern Stand. This had for its architect Mr Kenneth Peacock who had also designed the Warner Stand five years previously.

Diana Rait Kerr resigned as MCC's curator in 1968. With her departure from Lord's a link with the pre-war ground was lost because she had moved to the Secretary's official house in Elm Tree Road when her father was appointed to that post in 1936. On her retirement she joined forces with a person who was, to use E.W. Swanton's apt phrase, in a double sense a cricketer to his fingertips. With Ian Peebles she wrote a very valuable account of Lord's in the quarter of a century which had elapsed since the end of the Second World War. In 1969 the head groundsman, Ted Swannell, retired to be succeeded by Jim Farebrother whilst the tourists that year were the West Indians and the New Zealanders.

It was, however, for events which took place off the field that the closing years of the decade will be particularly remembered. The period between 1968 and 1970 especially was a far from tranquil one at the headquarters of the game. This was due to a great controversy over the desirability or otherwise of continuing cricketing links with South Africa. The apartheid policies of the government of that country were quite clearly in opposition to those of a multi-racial game – the question, however, was whether change would be more likely to be achieved through maintaining normal sporting links or through an outright boycott.

In particular the dispute centred at first on the non-selection of Basil d'Oliveira to go on the projected MCC tour of South Africa. This had been scheduled for the off-season of 1968/69. D'Oliveira had not on the whole enjoyed a very successful season in 1968, but he had made a tremendous comeback with a splendid century in The Oval Test against Australia. When Tom Cartwright had to

withdraw from the team, d'Oliveira was then chosen to join the touring party. The South African Government used this late selection to imply that the picking of Basil d'Oliveira had been made for political reasons and was not based on cricketing criteria. For that reason he would not be acceptable on the tour. MCC strongly denied that this was the case, but the club called off the tour when it became clear that the team in its entirety would not be welcome in South Africa.

The handling by MCC of this very sensitive situation was called into question and a special general meeting of members was held at Church House, Westminster, in December 1968. Strong words were uttered on both sides. The one bright note throughout this sad and unfortunate dispute was the very dignified bearing of Basil d'Oliveira.

A delicate situation was further complicated the following year when overall control of the game passed to a new body. This was called the Cricket Council and it comprised representatives of MCC, the Test and County Cricket Board and the National Cricket Association. The latter body was founded to represent at the highest administrative level the interests of cricket and cricketers at the grass roots. As a result of all these changes, the role of

Lord's pictured in 1969, showing the precautions taken to avoid any damage to the pitch by demonstrators.

The Grace Gates.

MCC has inevitably had to alter. It became more than ever before a private club with a private function.

Whilst these organisational changes were taking place the controversy over cricketing links with South Africa continued without a break. The wickets at Lord's were protected by searchlights and guarded with barbed wire. The presence of security dogs did little to lighten the general gloom and the sense of foreboding that prevailed. The South Africans were due to tour this country in 1970. To complicate matters even further the Prime Minister, Mr Harold Wilson, had just called a General Election. The very last thing that the Government would have wanted would have been to give to the electorate the impression that law and order had broken down in the country. In the event the Government in the person of the then Home Secretary, Mr James Callaghan, requested that the invitation to the South Africans to come to England that summer be withdrawn. There was a very justifiable fear that large-scale demonstrations would lead to public disorder. The cricketing authorities had little option but to agree to the Government's request to call off the tour. In the place of the expected Springboks, the Rest of the World side appeared at Lord's in 1970.

Many years later a lighter sequel to these momentous events took place. In 1994 South Africa made a very welcome comeback to the Test match scene at Lord's. A VIP guest of honour on that occasion was that country's Vice President, Mr Thabo Mbeki. A member of the MCC Committee, who was anxious to make some polite conversation, asked the distinguished guest if he had ever been to Lord's before. 'Oh yes,' replied Mr Mbeki, 'I used frequently to demonstrate here when I was a student at the University of Sussex.' It was not quite the reply that had been expected.

In 1972 the Benson & Hedges Cup (a second knockout competition) was inaugurated. Two years later Mr Jack Bailey, who had played for Oxford University and Essex, took over as Secretary of MCC. He was the first specialist in the increasingly important fields of public relations and marketing to have been recruited to the MCC Secretariat. He succeeded Billy Griffith, who had experienced what was almost certainly the most stressful period in office of all time. An example of this tension was the bomb scare that disrupted the West Indies Test of 1973. Mr Griffith had definitely earned his retirement.

In between these two events a pivotal figure retired from the employ of MCC. Dick Gaby left his post as Club Superintendent in 1973. His father (Richard Gaby Senior) had joined the Lord's staff 100 years earlier and the family was indeed a Lord's institution. If the President of MCC can be compared in military terms with the Colonel of the Regiment and if the Secretary can be likened to the Commanding Officer, then Dick Gaby's role was somewhat akin to a combination of Adjutant and Sergeant Major. His encyclopaedic knowledge of the place ensured that the nuts and bolts, which kept the complicated administration of Lord's together, were held very firmly in place. It was also a happy ship – Dick Gaby had a genuine concern for the welfare of individuals.

In 1975 Lord's was the scene for a most memorable final of the first World Cup for cricket. In a very tense finish the West Indies defeated Australia and accordingly

Veterans of the Lord's staff are presented to the Queen in 1971.
From left to right: Audrey Jones, G.M. (Joe) Gaby, Henry Johns,
Jim Farebrother and Charles Wray.

Ian Botham by Nick Botting.

received the trophy from the Duke of Edinburgh. Prince Philip was occupying the Presidency of MCC for a second term of office.

The MCC Annual Report said that the visiting Australian team 'were a fine all-round side, very capable, led by their captain, and had in D.K. Lillee a fast bowler of the highest class'.

The West Indians were the tourists in 1976 and were a very good team who easily beat England but the MCC side in India, however, were victorious the following winter under the captaincy of Tony Greig.

1977 saw the opening by Sir George Allen of the first indoor school at Lord's. This notable addition to the facilities at the game's headquarters was intended, as the inscription by the entrance to the building indicated, to help 'cricketers of every age and ability'.

The year was, however, dominated by the controversy caused by Mr Kerry Packer and his World Series Cricket. The Club's Annual Report commented in 1978, 'In their capacity as Chairman and Secretary of the International Cricket Conference, the President and Secretary shouldered an exceptionally heavy burden in grappling with the problem posed by the Packer organisation's challenge to the current system of international cricket. As defendants on behalf of the Conference in the ensuing legal action they were involved in innumerable consultations with counsel, the Secretary was in the witness box for some thirteen hours and the task of assembling evidence all over the world on the intricacies of cricket administration in the Test-Match playing countries was in itself formidable and demanding. The committee noted that one of its number, a Mr W.H. Webster, attended every session of the 31-day hearing brought by World Series Cricket.'

A break with the past occurred with the fact that England's overseas tour to Pakistan and New Zealand in 1977/78 was the first to dispense with the name of MCC as its official designation. The club explained in its Annual Report:

'During 1977 the Cricket Council accepted a proposal from the Test and County Cricket Board that in future touring teams should be described as "England". They felt that, with the present division of duties in English cricket, it might be misleading to retain MCC's name. The Club were gratified, however, to be asked for their agreement – which was freely given – to the retention of MCC's colours by overseas touring parties.'

Ian Botham was the hero in England's Test victories against both Pakistan and New Zealand at Lord's in 1978. In the former match he made 108 runs and took 8 second innings wickets. In the latter game he took 10 wickets in the match. 1979 saw the West Indies victorious in the World Cup. They defeated England by 92 runs in the final.

1980 witnessed the centenary of Test cricket in this country. Logically the main game to celebrate this notable anniversary should have been played at The Oval where the original fixture had taken place in 1980. It was, however, felt that more people would be able to be accommodated at Lord's. In the event the game was a splendid social occasion with a great reunion of English and Australian Test players taking place, but the match was most unfortunately badly affected by the weather. The outcome was that in strictly cricketing terms it was not a very noteworthy game – in this respect it was quite unlike the Centenary Test that had taken place in Melbourne three years previously. Perhaps the best long-term result of the match lay in the fact that the committee commissioned Arthur Weaver to paint a record of the scene and this was done to a very good effect.

In 1981 the National Westminster Bank took over the sponsorship of the Gillette Cup – one day championships had by this date become a firmly established part of the cricket scene.

In the Lord's Tests of 1982 England beat India but were defeated by Pakistan. A more memorable game than the Centenary Test match at Lord's was the final of the World Cup in 1983. India was to make cricketing history when

A group of England and Australian players, Centenary Test 1980.
(Photograph by Patrick Eagar.)

Dennis Lillee bowling and Geoff Boycott backing up in the Centenary
Test England *v.* Australia, 1980. (Photograph by Patrick Eagar.)

they defeated the much fancied West Indies side. The exuberant celebrations of the Indian supporters echoed round the environs of St John's Wood until the early hours of the morning. In addition a postage stamp was issued back in India to commemorate the event.

Off the field Mr John Carlisle, the Conservative Member of Parliament for Luton West, was the prime mover in requisitioning a Special General Meeting of MCC at Church House, Westminster on 13 July 1983. The resolution was that 'the members of MCC Committee implemented the selection of an MCC touring party to tour South Africa'. The committee opposed the resolution which was lost by 6,069 votes to 3,935.

During the next season Lord's was very glad to welcome another team from the Indian sub-continent. Sri Lanka made her Test debut at Lord's in a match in which Sidath Wettimuny excelled. He scored 190 in an outstanding innings. In the Test against Australia the following season of 1985, Allan Border (the visiting captain) scored 43 per cent of his victorious side's runs including a magnificent first innings score of 196.

On a more cerebral note 1985 witnessed the opening of the enlarged MCC Library in the tennis court block. The ceremony was performed by F.G. Mann, the then President of MCC. A new library was one way in which MCC was looking ahead towards the celebration of its forthcoming

England *v.* Australia, the Centenary Test Match by Arthur Weaver.

Fans invade the pitch after India's victory over the West Indies in the World Cup final in 1983. (Photograph by Patrick Eagar.)

200th birthday. Much thought went into the planning of this notable event in the annals of Lord's. One early beneficiary of the improved library facilities was Tony Lewis. His book, which was appropriately entitled *Double Century*, was the much-acclaimed official history of Lord's, which was commissioned by MCC. It was published to coincide with the bicentenary in 1987.

Meanwhile on the field of play England were saved by Graham Gooch from a possible defeat by New Zealand in the 1986 Lord's Test Match. Earlier in the season India defeated England by 5 wickets to notch up their first Test victory at the headquarters of the game.

The great bicentenary year of 1987 soon arrived but in the event the party atmosphere was not always prevalent during the forthcoming few months. Internal controversy tended to dominate the first half of the year. Further sadness was caused by the serious illness that assailed Colin Cowdrey, the President at the time. The weather too did not help. The first function of the bicentenary year took place on 13 January, the 155th anniversary of the death of Thomas Lord. In a raging blizzard, witnessed by the Bishop of Portsmouth, Colin Cowdrey

Kapil Dev and Mohinder Amarnath with the World Cup.
(Photograph by Patrick Eagar.)

F.G. Mann, President of MCC 1984-85, painted in 1995.

laid a wreath on the grave of the founder. It marked the start of the year's celebrations. It was a year of freak weather which culminated in the famous hurricane in the autumn. Earlier in the year the Bicentenary Ball at Lord's had hastily to be relocated when the marquee on the Nursery blew down in a mini-hurricane on the morning of the great event. A Dunkirk spirit prevailed, however, and the proceedings went ahead in the pavilion and on the floor of the tennis court.

At the beginning of 1987, Lt Col. John Stephenson became Acting Secretary of MCC. Later in the year he was confirmed in his post; he was thus able to master-mind the bicentenary celebrations which culminated in a grand finale with a great banquet in London's Guildhall. The main speaker was the former Prime Minister, Lord Home of the Hirsel who (as Lord Dunglass) had toured South America with the MCC team in 1926. The other major set piece was the match in August between MCC and the Rest of the World. By a nice piece of alliteration four batsmen whose names all began with a 'G' each made centuries. They were Gordon Greenidge, Graham Gooch, Mike Gatting and Sunil Gavaskar. The match took place in a heatwave – it was a pity that rain intervened on the final day.

A more permanent commemoration of the bicentenary was the completion of the much acclaimed Mound Stand. Its old predecessor was built in 1898/99. This edifice was gutted and the new fire-resistant seats were installed. Superimposed above the old stand was built the famous 'tented' structure designed by Sir Michael Hopkins. An architectural masterpiece had arrived at Lord's. It has indeed been given the rare accolade of being illustrated in Sir Nikolaus Pevsner's book on this area in his celebrated Penguin *Buildings of England* series.

In this way a great physical transformation of Lord's was commenced. Sir Nikolaus had previously said in an earlier volume that Lord's consisted of a jumble of buildings which had been erected without any aesthetic aspirations. Sir Nikolaus stated that this state of affairs would not have

Bicentenary programme, 1787-1987.

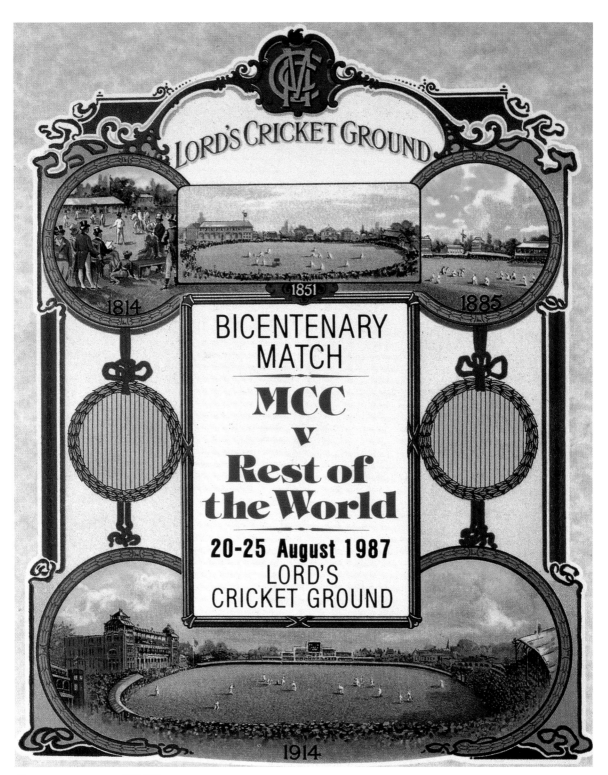

Bicentenary programme, 1787-1987.

been tolerated on the Continent. This stricture was not
entirely fair because several of the leading architects of the
day had made their individual contribution to the physical
appearance of the ground but the place perhaps lacked a
unity. Pevsner could not make a similar remark today,
however. Indeed the *Independent* went so far as to say that
Lord's was the centre for the most distinguished ensemble
of modern architecture in the entire country.

MCC *v.* Rest of the World, 1987, by William Bowyer RA.

Lord Home makes his speech at the MCC Bicentenary Dinner in the Guildhall. (Photograph by Patrick Eagar.)

1987 – 2003
MODERN TIMES

Aerial view of Lord's. (Photograph by Patrick Eagar.)

After the excitement of the bicentenary of MCC, life continued at Lord's on perhaps a more even keel. A piece of history was made in 1990 when the name of a great cricketing knight (Sir Richard Hadlee) appeared on the scoreboard. Another great performance for the record books was Graham Gooch's 333 runs which he scored in the Test match that year against India. His bat (which has been adorned with a painting by Jack Russell) is on display in the MCC Museum.

The present pavilion was opened on 1 May 1890. One hundred years to the day a party was held in the Long Room. This was attended by members of the families of Thomas Verity (the architect of the pavilion) and of Sir Spencer Ponsonby-Fane. The silver trowel which had been used to lay the foundation stone by Sir Spencer, as Treasurer of MCC back in 1890, was on display for the occasion. To coincide with this notable anniversary the Gestetner Tour of Lord's was launched. This was established to enable many more people to come to Lord's and to view the remarkable treasures in the MCC collection.

Two of Lord's favourite sons were commemorated in 1991 when the Compton and Edrich stands were opened to the public. These took the place of the old free seats. It was decided by the Committee that the new stands should not be built to too great a height. Lord's has thus remained on a human scale and avoided becoming too much of a stadium. The view of the trees which can be observed from the Long Room has been jealously preserved – this has doubtless been to the relief of many members.

At the end of 1993 Colonel John Stephenson retired. He had taken over the reins at a difficult moment in the club's history and by his genial manner and with his concern for individuals he endeared himself to one and all and helped to leave the club in very fine order. Mr Roger Knight resigned from his post as Headmaster of Worksop College to take over the Secretaryship of MCC. Lord's thus was fortunate to gain the services of an administrator who had not only had great experience as a county cricketer but was also one who was well versed in the world of education. In Mr Knight's first summer at Lord's the New Zealand Test was drawn but South Africa, who were making a most welcome return to the Test Match arena at the headquarters of cricket, were victorious by the very decisive margin of 356 runs.

Graham Gooch, 1992. Portrait by Ishbel Myerscough.

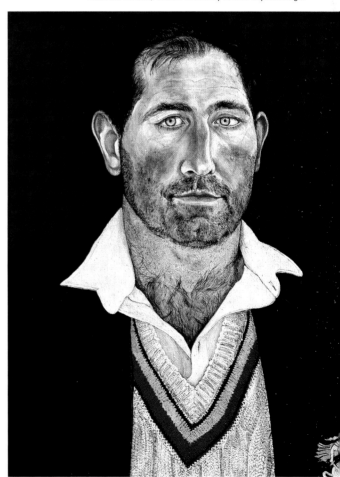

Graham Gooch's bat, featuring an illustration
by Jack Russell.

Building work in progress on the Compton and Edrich Stands.

Decorative work on the Pavilion turrets. (Photograph by James Finlay)

Overleaf: Conversation Piece by Andrew Festing. From left to right, portraits (deceased players): W.J. Edrich, K.F. Barrington, Sir Leonard Hutton, J.C. Laker. Foreground: T.G. Evans, T.E. Bailey, P.B.H. May, J.B. Statham, D.C.S. Compton, A.V. Bedser, M.C. Cowdrey, F.S. Trueman, E.R. Dexter, T.W. Graveney. This was commissioned by MCC in 1993.

Commemorative stained glass window in the MCC Museum.

Ducks venture out during the Second Test, England *v.* Australia at Lord's
in 1993. (Photograph by Patrick Eagar.)

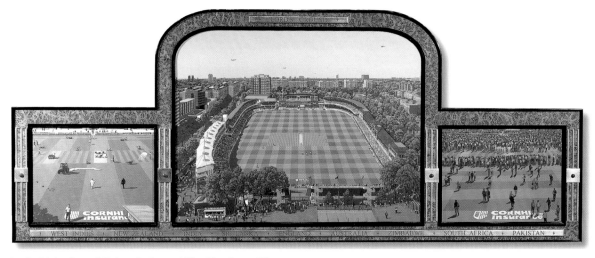

Lord's Cricket Ground: Before, During and After Play, Second Test,
England *v.* West Indies. Triptych by Jonathan Warrender, 1995.

England won the 1995 Lord's Test against the West Indies by a margin of 72 runs. This was due to magnificent bowling by Dominic Cork in the second innings. His analysis of 7 for 43 was the best by any England player on his Test debut and fifth on the list for any country. A splendid new facility was launched in 1995 when the Duke of Edinburgh opened the new Indoor School. It replaced the 1977 building that had proved its worth but which, to put it mildly, had no very great claims to architectural merit. Mr David Morley was the architect of the new school.

The 1996 Test Match against India was drawn but the later game versus Pakistan was lost by 164 runs. In 1997 England were lucky to draw the Test against Australia after the home team only made 77 in their first innings. Perhaps it was more significant that in the same year MCC launched its own site on the Internet. In the realm of administration the game's governing bodies amalgamated in 1997 to form the England and Wales Cricket Board (which is usually abbreviated to the initials E.C.B.).

1998 was a momentous year at Lord's. Amongst other things it witnessed the completion of the new Grandstand. A great number of people were sorry to see the last of Sir Herbert Baker's handsome predecessor but the latter possessed too many seats which only had a restricted view of

The new MCC Indoor Cricket School is opened by HRH Prince Philip.
(Photograph by Patrick Eagar.)

Conversation Piece by Andrew Festing. From left to right, standing:
J.A. Snow, B.L. d'Oliveira, A.P.E. Knott, D.L. Underwood. Seated:
J.H. Edrich, F.J. Titmus, D.B. Close, G. Boycott, R. Illingworth,
D.L. Amiss, M.J.K. Smith. This was commissioned in 1997.

Right: Lesley Garrett in the Long Room.
(Photograph by Patrick Eagar.)

Below: The Long Room. (Photograph by Patrick Eagar.)

Building work on the new Grand Stand.
(Photograph by Bill Smith.)

Overleaf: Balloons are released to mark the launch of the 1999 World Cup.
(Photograph by James Finlay.)

the play and it had proved more and more inadequate for the changing and demanding needs of modern use. On the other hand it had only cost a mere £46,000 to build back in 1926. Its successor turned out to be somewhat more expensive incurring, as it did, expenditure in the region of £14,000,000.

A special match marked the 150th anniversary of the birth of Dr W.G. Grace. Invited to this game were as many of the descendants of W.G. as could be located. The proceeds went to the Diana, Princess of Wales Memorial Fund. A short sequel was shown on the big screen depicting W.G. on his fiftieth birthday, exactly 100 years earlier on 18 July 1898. In the MCC Museum there was held a special exhibition on the life of W.G. This was opened by his last surviving grandchild, Mrs Primrose Worthington. She was almost certainly the only person alive in 1998 who had known W.G. well. She took part in a memorable conversation with her fellow nonagenarian, E.W. (Jim) Swanton, the veteran cricket writer, on that occasion.

England deservedly lost to South Africa in the 1998 Lord's Test. Extras were top 'scorer' at 20 in England's first innings total of 110. More significantly, at the end of the season the decision was eventually reached to admit women into membership of MCC. Ten ladies were shortly after elected as Honorary Members. They had one and all rendered very distinguished services to the game. Had not W.G. himself owed a great deal to the early coaching that had been given to him by his mother, Mrs Martha Grace?

Another new facility was built to meet the demands of the 1999 World Cup. A magnificent Media Centre was commissioned by MCC and largely sponsored by the National Westminster Bank. It was designed by naval architects and was made of aluminium. It was indeed the prototype for its particular method of construction. Together with the erection of a nursery pavilion to meet the demands of corporate hospitality in particular, the Nursery End at Lord's could match the rest of the ground and boast of a splendid collection of new and exciting buildings.

Colin Cowdrey, Mrs Worthington and E.W. Swanton.
(Photograph by Bill Smith.)

Below: The theatre at Lord's, 1998.
Bottom: The New Invincibles by David Buckland (commissioned by MCC in 2001).

Michael Atherton by Andy Pankhurst, 2000.

Alec Stewart by Andy Pankhurst, 2000.

Work in progress on the new Compton and Edrich Stands.
(Photograph by Bill Smith.)

The semi-final of the World Cup had resulted in a tie at Edgbaston between Australia and South Africa. Unfortunately the final at Lord's was not especially memorable. Australia defeated Pakistan by eight wickets but *Wisden* implied that the margin should have been even greater – Pakistan were in truth outplayed. The Test against New Zealand later in the season at Lord's resulted in England losing to the Kiwis for the first time ever at the home of cricket.

2000 saw a new code of the Laws of Cricket. It contained an important preamble on the spirit of cricket. This began:

'Cricket is a game that owes much of its unique appeal to the fact that it should be played not only within its Laws, but also within the Spirit of the Game. Any action that is seen to abuse the spirit causes injury to the game itself. The major responsibility for ensuring the spirit of fair play rests with the captains.'

MCC was very keen to follow in the footsteps of Lord Cowdrey who was most anxious to promote better standards of behaviour at all levels of the game and who was so sadly to die at the end of 2000. England met Zimbabwe for the first time in a Lord's Test that year. The home side were triumphant by a margin of an innings and 209 runs.

The same year witnessed the 100th Lord's Test. This was the England *v.* West Indies game. Appropriately it was an amazing match. To quote *Wisden* – 'Many talk of the Lord's Test of 1963 as being the apogee between these two

Inside the Media Centre.

The new Natwest Media Centre, pictured in 1999 during the 2nd Cornhill
Test England *v*. New Zealand. (Photograph by Patrick Eagar.)

A panoramic view of Lord's cricket ground. (Photograph by Patrick Eagar.)

Father Time, pictured in 1997. (Photograph by Patrick Eagar.)

The balcony on the pavilion. (Photograph by James Finlay)

sides, but for sheer drama and sustained excitement this one may have usurped it.' On the second day of the Test wickets fell with such great speed that parts of all four innings were played before nightfall even though some of the proceedings were interrupted by rain. The visiting side only made 54 in their second innings – this was the West Indies' third lowest total and their worst against England.

The third day was equally full of excitement and almost to the very end no fewer than four results were possible. In fading light England came near the West Indies total. Finally Dominic Cork drove Courtney Walsh through the covers to ensure an England victory by the close margin of two wickets.

One of these 100 Tests was the Australia *v.* South Africa fixture in the Triangular series of 1912. The 100th England Test match at Lord's was the game against Pakistan a year later in 2001. The home side won this fixture by an innings and nine runs. The Test match against Australia later that year, however, resulted in a defeat by eight wickets. *Wisden* says that the tourists had a 'display of all-round brilliance that approached perfection'.

In 2002 the Test match against Sri Lanka was drawn. For the first time in the history of English cricket no umpire from the home country stood in a Test match played at Lord's. The Test against India resulted in an England win by 170 runs. The match was a great triumph for Nasser Hussain, the England captain. He scored 155 in his first innings. Michael Vaughan and John Crawley also made centuries. In the closing months of 2002, Lord's looked, in the words of the Secretary and Chief Executive, rather like Weston-super-Mare with the tide out. The turf was removed in a complicated operation to improve the drainage. Fortunately, the weather was kind and by Christmas all had been replaced and Lord's was ready to face the future with confidence.

We have seen that MCC is one of the oldest of the London clubs. Lord's has been an integral part of the capital scene for considerably longer than Trafalgar Square. Much has changed on the ground, however. If one looks at the painting of Lord's, which Charles Cundall executed in 1938, one finds that only the pavilion area is recognisable today. The essential nature of the place remains the same, nonetheless. One can but hope that the founder, Thomas Lord, and his patron, the Earl of Winchilsea, would feel at home were they to return to the ground which they established because Lord's is indeed eternal in its appeal to cricketers and to all lovers of our great national game.

Conversation Piece by Andrew Festing. From left to right: J.E. Emburey,
G.A. Gooch, D.I. Gower, M.W. Gatting, A.W. Greig, R.W. Taylor,
A.J. Lamb, J.M. Brearley, R.G.D. Willis, D.W. Randall. The author has
inveigled his way into the picture and is seated in front of the open
window. This was commissioned by MCC in 2000.

Above and Below: Relaying the turf on the outfield at Lord's, autumn 2002.
(Photographs by Patrick Eagar.)

Lord's in the snow, January 2003. (Photograph by Patrick Eagar.)

BIBLIOGRAPHY

Of the making of books on Lord's there is no end. The following are perhaps the most important:

Niall Edworthy: *Lord's: The Home of Cricket* (Virgin Books, 1999)

Lord Harris & F.A. Ashley-Cooper: *Lord's and the MCC* (London & Counties Press Association, 1914)

Tony Lewis: *Double Century* (Hodder & Stoughton, 1987)

Geoffrey Moorhouse: *Lord's* (Hodder & Stoughton, 1983)

Diana Rait Kerr & Ian Peebles: *Lord's 1946-1970* (Harrap, 1971)

Jonathan Rice: *One Hundred Lord's Tests* (Methuen, 2001)

A.D. Taylor: *Annals of Lord's and History of the MCC* (J.W. Arrowsmith, 1903)

The Times: MCC 1787-1937 (The Times, 1937)

P.F. Warner: *Lord's – 1787-1945* (Harrap, 1946)

ACKNOWLEDGEMENTS

My debts are agreeably large and numerous. First, I must thank the MCC Arts and Library Sub-Committee, under the Chairmanship of Lord Fellowes, for giving me the go-ahead to do this work. In particular, I am grateful to the Publishing Working Party for their support – especially I should like to mention Mr Hubert Doggart, Dr Gerald Howat, Mr David Rayvern Allen, Mr Jonathan Rice and Mr John Woodcock.

My thanks further go to the Secretary and Chief Executive of MCC, Mr Roger Knight, for his permission to proceed. I also owe a great debt to his predecessor, the late Lt-Col. John Stephenson, whose support of a very unmilitary Curator was inspirational. Mr Tony Lewis has been another source of encouragement and help.

I have owed much to my more immediate colleagues, both past and present. My predecessor, Diana Rait Kerr, set a standard which I have not been able to match but which has always been my example. My former colleagues, the late Denis Rons, the late Fay Ashmore, Edward Holland, Michael Lucy and June Bayliss all helped me with my cricketing education. My present assistants, Glenys Williams, Michael Wolton and Ken Daldry, have been a great support.

The late Geoffrey Copinger was always ready to lend me rare publications, whilst Irving Rosenwater has the enviable gift of being able to unscrew the unscrutable.

In more specific areas I have been grateful for information supplied by the Revd Prebendary John Slater, the former vicar of St John's Wood, and Dr Neil Young of the Imperial War Museum. I am particularly indebted to Marina Warner for her permission to quote from the book on Lord's which was written by her grandfather, the late Sir Pelham Warner.

My final words of gratitude must go to Philip Bailey for his most comprehensive statistical appendix, to my publishers for their patience in dealing with a tardy wordsmith (and in particular to James Howarth), and then to members of my family. My brother, Dudley, has marked the proofs with a schoolmasterly pen whilst my sister, Mrs Rosemary Ratcliff, has always put the kettle on when I arrived back home on the Isle of Wight in order to find a sense of peace and sanity. It is to her I dedicate this book, although I think it is some time now since she last glanced at a page of *Wisden*.

Stephen Green
Lord's
August 2003

G.A. Gooch in action. (Photograph by Patrick Eagar.)

STATISTICS

Number in brackets after year indicates the position of the particular Test within the rubber. For example, 2003 (2) would denote the Second Test of the summer against that opposition.

DOUBLE HUNDREDS

333	G.A. Gooch	England	India	1990 (1)
316★	J.B. Hobbs	Surrey	Middlesex	1926
315★	P. Holmes	Yorkshire	Middlesex	1925
315	M.A. Wagh	Warwickshire	Middlesex	2001
281★	W.H. Ponsford	Australians	MCC	1934
278	D.G. Bradman	Australians	MCC	1938
278	W. Ward	MCC	Norfolk	1820
277★	E.H. Hendren	Middlesex	Kent	1922
265	A.D. Brown	Surrey	Middlesex	1999
261★	J.D. Carr	Middlesex	Glos	1994
260	K.S. Ranjitsinhji	Sussex	MCC	1897
259	G.C. Smith	South Africa	England	2003 (2)
255★	D.L. Haynes	Middlesex	Sussex	1990
254	D.G. Bradman	Australia	England	1930 (2)
252★	D.C.S Compton	Middlesex	Somerset	1948
251	M.L. Love	Durham	Middlesex	2002
248★	W.W. Armstrong	Australians	G of England	1905
248★	W.N. Slack	Middlesex	Worcs	1981
245	W.J. Edrich	Middlesex	Notts	1938
243★	H.W. Lee	Middlesex	Notts	1921
241★	J.L. Langer	Middlesex	Kent	1999
240	W.R. Hammond	England	Australia	1938 (2)
238★	Nawab of Pataudi	Oxford	Cambridge	1931
235	D.C.S. Compton	Middlesex	Surrey	1946
234★	J.W. Hearne	Middlesex	Somerset	1911
234	E.H. Hendren	Middlesex	Worcs	1925
233★	J.L. Langer	Middlesex	Somerset	1998
233	G.L. Jessop	Rest of England	Yorkshire	1901
233	M.R. Ramprakash	Middlesex	Surrey	1992
232★	S.M. Brown	Middlesex	Somerset	1951
232★	C.B. Fry	Gentlemen	Players	1903
232	E.H. Hendren	Middlesex	Notts	1920
229	J.D.B. Robertson	Middlesex	Hampshire	1947
228	W. Gunn	Players	Australians	1890
228	E.S.B. Williams	Army	Royal Navy	1928
227	G.A. Headley	West Indians	Middlesex	1939
226	B.C. Lara	Warwickshire	Middlesex	1998
225	R.N. Harvey	Australians	MCC	1956
224★	M.W. Gatting	Middlesex	England 'A'	1994

224★	A. Shrewsbury	Notts	Middlesex	1885
224	S.W. Scott	Middlesex	Glos	1892
224	V.J. Wells	Leicestershire	Middlesex	1997
221	A.E. Stoddart	Middlesex	Somerset	1900
218★	J.W. Hearne	Middlesex	Hampshire	1919
217	W.H. Hadow	Middlesex	MCC	1871
216	M.W. Gatting	Middlesex	New Zealand	1983
215★	M.W. Gatting	Middlesex	Derbyshire	1991
214★	D.C.S. Compton	Middlesex	Derbyshire	1939
214★	C.G. Greenidge	West Indies	England	1984 (2)
214	E.H. Hendren	MCC	Yorkshire	1919
214	M.R. Ramprakash	Middlesex	Surrey	1995
213	E.H. Hendren	Middlesex	Yorkshire	1926
212	A. Shrewsbury	Notts	Middlesex	1892
211	W.J. Edrich	Middlesex	Essex	1953
211	G. Goonesena	Cambridge	Oxford	1957
211	J.B. Hobbs	England	South Africa	1924 (2)
210★	R.J. Hadlee	Notts	Middlesex	1984
210	M.W. Gatting	Middlesex	Notts	1988
209★	J.T. Bell	Wales	MCC	1927
209★	M.R. Ramprakash	Middlesex	Surrey	1999
208	D.C.S. Compton	England	South Africa	1947 (2)
206★	W.A. Brown	Australia	England	1938 (2)
206	M.P. Donnelly	New Zealand	England	1949 (2)
206	E.T. Killick	Middlesex	Warwickshire	1931
205★	J. Hardstaff	England	India	1946 (1)
205	M.R. Ramprakash	Middlesex	Sussex	1995
204	J.W. Hearne	Middlesex	Lancashire	1914
204	P.F. Warner	MCC	Sussex	1905
203	J.T. Brown	Yorkshire	Middlesex	1896
203	W. Gunn	MCC	Yorkshire	1885
203	E.H. Hendren	Middlesex	Northants	1931
203	A.E. Knight	Leicestershire	MCC	1904
202	E.H. Hendren	MCC	Surrey	1936
202	J.B. Hobbs	Surrey	Yorkshire	1914
201★	G. Boycott	Yorkshire	Middlesex	1975
201★	J.D.B. Robertson	Middlesex	Essex	1957
201★	W.N. Slack	Middlesex	Australians	1985
201★	M.J.K. Smith	Oxford	Cambridge	1954

201★	M.M. Walford	Oxford	MCC	1938
201	F.H. Gillingham	Essex	Middlesex	1904
201	E.H. Hendren	Middlesex	Hampshire	1919
201	A. Ratcliffe	Cambridge	Oxford	1931
200★	K.R. Brown	Middlesex	Notts	1990
200★	A.L. Hassett	Australians	G of England	1948
200	E.H. Hendren	Middlesex	Hampshire	1928
200	Majid Khan	Cambridge	Oxford	1970
200	Mohsin Khan	Pakistan	England	1982 (2)
200	F.A. Tarrant	Middlesex	Worcs	1914

TWO HUNDREDS IN A MATCH

W.H. Ashdown	121 & 103	Kent v. Middlesex	1931
B.J. Booth	109 & 104	Leics v. Middlesex	1965
B.J.T. Bosanquet	136 & 139	Middlesex v. Leics	1900
B.J.T. Bosanquet	103 & 100★	Middlesex v. Sussex	1905
R.J. Boyd-Moss	139 & 124	Cambridge v. Oxford	1983
R.J. Christiani	131★& 100★	W Indies v. Middlesex	1950
M.J. Di Venuto	192★& 113	Derbyshire v. Middlesex	2002
K.S. Duleepsinhji	116 & 102★	Sussex v. Middlesex	1930
K.S. Duleepsinhji	125 & 103★	Gentlemen v. Players	1930
H.J. Enthoven	123 & 115	Middlesex v. Sussex	1930
R.E. Foster	102★& 136	Gentlemen v. Players	1900
C.B. Fry	156 & 106	Sussex v. MCC	1905
G.A. Gooch	333 & 123	England v. India	1990 (1)
W.R. Hammond	121 & 102	England v. Dominions	1945
D.L. Haynes	181 & 129	Middlesex v. N Zealand	1990
G.A. Headley	106 & 107	West Indies v. England	1939 (1)
J.W. Hearne	104 & 101★	Middlesex v. Glamorgan	1931
E.H. Hendren	101 & 101	Middlesex v. Kent	1933
E.H. Hendren	104 & 101	Middlesex v. Surrey	1936
J.H. King	104 & 109★	Players v. Gentlemen	1904
W. Lambert	107★& 157	Sussex v. Epsom	1817
H.W. Lee	124 & 105★	Middlesex v. Lancashire	1929
P.H. Parfitt	122 & 114	Middlesex v. Pakistanis	1962
P.A. Perrin	140 & 103★	Essex v. Middlesex	1905
J.D.B. Robertson	147 & 137	Middlesex v. Sussex	1948
W.N. Slack	163★& 105★	Middlesex v. Glamorgan	1988
A.E. Stoddart	195★ & 124	Middlesex v. Notts	1893

LONGEST INNINGS

636 mins	S. Wettimuny	190	Sri Lanka v. England	1984
630 mins	M.A. Waugh	315	Warks v. Middlesex	2001
627 mins	G.A. Gooch	333	England v. India	1990 (1)

MOST RUNS IN A CAREER

25473	E.H. Hendren
16853	D.C.S. Compton
16466	W.J. Edrich
16214	J.W. Hearne
15408	J.D.B. Robertson
14110	P.F. Warner

UNUSUAL DISMISSALS

handled the ball	J. Grundy	MCC v. Kent	1857
handled the ball	A. Rees	Glamorgan v. Middlesex	1965
hit the ball twice	R.G. Barlow	North v. South	1878
hit the ball twice	H.E. Bull	MCC v. Oxford Univ	1864

HIGHEST PARTNERSHIPS

1ST WICKET

367★	G.D. Barlow/W.N. Slack	Middlesex v. Kent	1981
312	W.E. Russell/M.J. Harris	Middlesex v. Pakistan	1967
310	J.D.B. Robertson/S.M. Brown	Middlesex v. Notts	1947
301	D.L. Amiss/J.M. Brearley	MCC v. Leics	1976

2ND WICKET

380	F.A. Tarrant/J.W. Hearne	Middlesex v. Lancs	1914
314	H.W. Lee/E.H. Hendren	Middlesex v. Hants	1928

3RD WICKET

424	W.J. Edrich/D.C.S. Compton	Middlesex v. Somerset	1948
389	W.H. Ponsford/S.J. McCabe	Australians v. MCC	1934
370	W.J. Edrich/D.C.S. Compton	England v. S Africa	1947 (2)
318	C.T. Radley/M.W. Gatting	Middlesex v. NZ	1983
309★	C.B. Fry/A.C. MacLaren	Gentlemen v. Players	1903
308	G.A. Gooch/A.J. Lamb	England v. India	1990 (1)
304	W.J. Edrich/D.C.S. Compton	Middlesex v. Glos	1938
301	H. Sutcliffe/M. Leyland	Yorkshire v. Middlesex	1939

4TH WICKET

330	W. Barnes/W. Gunn	MCC v. Yorkshire	1885
325	J.W. Hearne/E.H. Hendren	Middlesex v. Hants	1919
304	D.C.S. Compton/F.G. Mann	Middlesex v. Surrey	1947

5TH WICKET

289★	N of Pataudi/L.E.G. Ames	England v. Rest	1934
288	A.D. Brown/A.J. Hollioake	Surrey v. Middlesex	1999

6TH WICKET

274★	G.S. Sobers/D.A.J. Holford	W. Indies v. England	1966 (2)
270	J.D. Carr/P.N. Weekes	Middlesex v. Glos	1994

7TH WICKET

289	G. Goonesena/G.W. Cook	Cambridge v. Oxford	1957
273★	W.W. Armstrong/J. Darling	Australians v. Gentlemen	1905
264	J.D. Carr/P.N. Weekes	Middlesex v. Somerset	1994

8TH WICKET

246	L.E.G. Ames/G.O.B. Allen	England v. N Zealand	1931

9TH WICKET

156	T.W. Hayward/J.T. Hearne	Players v. Gentlemen	1896
150	H. Philipson/A.C.M. Croome	Oxford v. MCC	1889

10TH WICKET

230	R.W. Nicholls/W. Roche	Middlesex v. Kent	1899
157	J.T. Parnham/J. White	North v. South	1886

BEST BOWLING IN AN INNINGS

W	R			
10	?	E. Hinkly	Kent *v.* England	1848
10	?	J. Wisden	North *v.* South	1850
10	38	S.E. Butler	Oxford *v.* Cambridge	1871
10	40	G.O.B. Allen	Middlesex *v.* Lancashire	1929
10	40	G.F. Tarrant	England *v.* Kent	1863
10	73	A. Shaw	MCC *v.* North	1874
10	90	A. Fielder	Players *v.* Gentlemen	1906
9	?	G.B. Lee	Oxford *v.* Cambridge	1839
9	?	F.W. Lillywhite	Players *v.* Gentlemen	1837
9	?	F.W. Lillywhite	Slow *v.* Fast Bowlers	1841
9	?	A. Mynn	Kent *v.* England	1842
9	?	T. Nixon	MCC *v.* Middlesex	1851
9	?	J. Wisden	Under 36 *v.* Over 36	1850
9	20	W.G. Grace	MCC *v.* Notts	1885
9	27	J. Jackson	Kent *v.* England	1858
9	28	A. Woodcock	Leicestershire *v.* MCC	1899
9	29	James Lillywhite jnr	Sussex *v.* MCC	1862
9	30	T. Hayward	England *v.* Kent	1860
9	30	J. Southerton	South *v.* North	1875
9	37	G. Wootton	MCC *v.* Oxford	1865
9	38	R.C. Robertson-Glasgow	Somerset *v.* Middlesex	1924
9	41	J.T. Hearne	MCC *v.* Notts	1892
9	43	J.T. Hearne	MCC *v.* Lancashire	1894
9	44	A.E.E. Vogler	MCC *v.* West Indians	1906
9	45	G. Wootton	MCC *v.* England	1868
9	46	J.W.A. Stephenson	Gentlemen *v.* Players	1936
9	48	C.L. Townsend	Glos *v.* Middlesex	1898
9	57	F.J. Titmus	Middlesex *v.* Lancs	1964
9	59	A.H. Evans	England XI *v.* R Daft's American XI	1880
9	59	T.W. Foster	Yorkshire *v.* MCC	1894
9	59	F.A. Tarrant	Middlesex *v.* Notts	1907
9	62	H. Verity	Yorkshire *v.* MCC	1939
9	64	C.D.B. Marsham	Gentlemen *v.* MCC	1855
9	65	J.J. Warr	Middlesex *v.* Kent	1956
9	69	G.H. Hirst	Yorkshire *v.* MCC	1912
9	71	J.T. Hearne	MCC *v.* Yorkshire	1900
9	71	M.W. Tate	Sussex *v.* Middlesex	1926
9	72	W. Wright	Kent *v.* MCC	1889
9	73	J.T. Hearne	MCC *v.* Australians	1896
9	78	M. Flanagan	MCC *v.* Surrey	1876
9	82	J.W. Hearne	Middlesex *v.* Surrey	1911
9	88	R. Lipscomb	Kent *v.* MCC	1871
9	97	C. Blythe	Kent *v.* Surrey	1914
9	105	J.W.H.T. Douglas	Gentlemen *v.* Players	1914
9	107	B.J.T. Bosanquet	MCC *v.* South Africans	1904
9	111	R.A. Sinfield	Glos *v.* Middlesex	1936

Note: F.W. Lillywhite took 10 wickets in an innings for Players *v.* Gentlemen in 1837, but there were 18 players on the Gentlemen's team

BEST BOWLING IN A MATCH

W	R			
16	?	E. Hinkly	Kent *v.* England	1848
16	52	J. Southerton	South *v.* North	1875
16	60	W.G. Grace	MCC *v.* Notts	1885
16	93	C.D.B. Marsham	Gentlemen *v.* MCC	1855
16	98	G.F. Tarrant	England *v.* Kent	1863
16	137	R.A.L. Massie	Australia *v.* England	1972 (2)
15	?	F.W. Lillywhite	England *v.* Kent	1840
15	47	F.A. Tarrant	Middlesex *v.* Hants	1913
15	49	T. Hayward	England *v.* Kent	1860
15	68	F.W. Tate	Sussex *v.* Middlesex	1902
15	91	J. Jackson	North *v.* South	1857
15	93	J.T. Hearne	Middlesex *v.* Somerset	1904
15	95	S.E. Butler	Oxford *v.* Cambridge	1871
15	97	J.C. Laker	Surrey *v.* MCC	1954
15	104	H. Verity	England *v.* Australia	1934 (2)
15	122	A.P. Freeman	Kent *v.* Middlesex	1933
15	134	C.L. Townsend	Glos *v.* Middlesex	1898
15	187	A.E. Trott	Middlesex *v.* Sussex	1901
15	189	A.R. Litteljohn	Middlesex *v.* Lancs	1911

Note: F.W. Lillywhite took 18 wickets in the match for Players *v.* Gentlemen in 1837, but there were 18 players on the Gentlemen's team

FOUR WICKETS IN FOUR BALLS

J.B. Hide	Sussex *v.* MCC		1890
F. Martin	MCC *v.* Derbyshire		1895
A.E. Trott	Middlesex *v.* Somerset		1907

Note: Trott also took another hat-trick in the same innings

MOST BALLS BOWLED IN AN INNINGS

B	ANALYSIS			
465	93-33-134-3	J.J. Ferris	Australians *v.* Players	1890
462	77-13-132-8	P.H. Edmonds	Middlesex *v.* Glos	1977
456	114-72-85-3	A. Watson	Lancs *v.* MCC	1884

MOST BALLS BOWLED IN A MATCH

B	ANALYSIS			
696	116-75-127-7	A.L. Valentine	West Indies *v.* England	1950 (2)
690	115-70-152-11	S. Ramadhin	West Indies *v.* England	1950 (2)

MOST WICKETS IN A CAREER

1724	J.T. Hearne
1191	F.J. Titmus
986	A.E. Trott
890	J.W. Hearne
709	F.A. Tarrant
708	J.M. Sims

100 RUNS & 10 WICKETS IN A MATCH

G.O.B. Allen	38, 104*/7–120, 3–36	
	MCC *v.* New Zealand	1927
W.W. Armstrong	55, 50*/3–20, 8–50	
	Australians *v.* Middlesex	1905
R.H.B. Bettington	28, 95/4–87, 6–78	
	Middlesex *v.* Sussex	1928
B.J.T. Bosanquet	103, 100*/3–75, 8–53	
	Middlesex *v.* Sussex	1905
F.M. Buckland	104/4–14, 6–53	
	Oxford University *v.* Middlesex	1877
W.G. Grace	134*/6–50, 4–31	
	Gentlemen *v.* Players	1868
W.G. Grace	7, 152/7–64, 5–61	
	Gentlemen *v.* Players	1875
W.G. Grace	89, 35/5–64, 7–92	
	Gloucestershire *v.* Middlesex	1883
R.J. Gregory	171/5–36, 5–66	
	Surrey *v.* Middlesex	1930
J.W. Hearne	88, 37*/5–78, 5–91	
	Middlesex *v.* Essex	1914
J.W. Hearne	79, 28/6–74, 4–73	
	Middlesex *v.* Notts	1922
J.W. Hearne	140, 57*/6–83, 6–45	
	Middlesex *v.* Sussex	1923
J.W. Hearne	14, 93/5–38, 6–36	
	Middlesex *v.* Gloucestershire	1924
G.H. Hirst	86, 18*/7–55, 4–28	
	Yorkshire *v.* MCC	1901
A.E. Trott	64, 69/6–57, 5–56	
	MCC *v.* Sussex	1899
A.E. Trott	123, 35*/6–132, 6–68	
	Middlesex *v.* Sussex	1899

MOST DISMISSALS IN AN INNINGS

8	S.A. Marsh	8 ct	Kent *v.* Middlesex	1991
7	W.F.F. Price	7 ct	Middlesex *v.* Yorkshire	1937
6	J. Barnard	2 ct, 4 st	MCC *v.* Godalming	1822
6	L.H. Compton	4 ct, 2 st	Middlesex *v.* Essex	1953
6	W. Lambert	3 ct, 3 st	MCC *v.* Hampshire	1816
6	J.T. Murray	6 ct	Middlesex *v.* Hampshire	1965
6	J.T. Murray	6 ct	England *v.* India	1967 (2)
6	W.F.F. Price	6 ct	Middlesex *v.* Warks	1938
6	G.R. Stephenson	5 ct, 1 st	Hampshire *v.* Middlesex	1976

MOST DISMISSALS IN A MATCH

9	J. Barnard	2 ct, 7 st	MCC *v.* Godalming	1822
9	G.R.A. Langley	8 ct, 1 st	Australia *v.* England	1956 (2)
9	S.A. Marsh	9 ct	Kent *v.* Middlesex	1991
9	J.T. Murray	8 ct, 1 st	Middlesex *v.* Hampshire	1965
9	A.E. Newton	6 ct, 3 st	Somerset *v.* Middlesex	1901

MOST CATCHES IN A INNINGS (FIELD)

6	A.J. Webbe	Gentlemen *v.* Players	1877
5	R.O. Butcher	Middlesex *v.* Australians	1981
5	F.G.J. Ford	Cambridge *v.* MCC	1888
5	N.E. Haig	Middlesex *v.* Notts	1928
5	L. Hutton	Players *v.* Gentlemen	1952

MOST CATCHES IN A MATCH (FIELD)

7	A.F.J. Ford	Middlesex *v.* Glos	1882
7	R.E. Foster	Oxford *v.* MCC	1898
6	W. Chatterton	Derbyshire *v.* MCC	1895
6	M.C. Cowdrey	England *v.* West Indies	1963 (2)
6	W.J. Edrich	Middlesex *v.* Surrey	1949
6	G.A. Gooch	Essex *v.* Middlesex	1985
6	W.G. Grace	MCC *v.* Yorkshire	1873
6	A.J. Lamb	England *v.* New Zealand	1983 (3)
6	C.A. Milton	Gloucestershire *v.* Middlesex	1953
6	G.S. Sobers	West Indies *v.* England	1973 (3)
6	G.F. Vernon	Middlesex *v.* Notts	1888
6	A.J. Webbe	Gentlemen *v.* Players	1877

HIGHEST INNINGS TOTAL

729–6 dec.	Australia *v.* England	1930 (2)
682–6 dec.	South Africa *v.* England	2003 (2)
665	West Indians *v.* Middlesex	1939
653–4 dec.	England *v.* India	1990 (1)
652–8 dec.	West Indies *v.* England	1973 (3)
645–6 dec.	Durham *v.* Middlesex	2002
632–4 dec.	Australia *v.* England	1993 (2)
631–9 dec.	Warwickshire *v.* Middlesex	2001
629	England *v.* India	1974 (2)
612–8 dec.	Middlesex *v.* Notts	1921
610–5 dec.	Australians *v.* Gentlemen	1948
609–8 dec.	Cambridge *v.* MCC	1913
608–7 dec.	Middlesex *v.* Hampshire	1919
607	MCC *v.* Cambridge	1902
602–7 dec.	Middlesex *v.* Sussex	1995

Note: MCC scored 735–9 dec. *v.* Wiltshire in 1888 in a minor match

LOWEST INNINGS TOTAL

15	MCC *v.* Surrey	1839
16	MCC *v.* Surrey	1872
17	G. of Kent *v.* G. of England	1850
18	The Bs *v.* England	1831
18	Australians *v.* MCC	1896
19	MCC *v.* Australians	1878
20	Middlesex *v.* MCC	1864
21	Kent *v.* England	1834
21	Notts *v.* MCC	1891
23	Sussex *v.* MCC	1838
23	Sussex *v.* MCC	1856
24	Middlesex *v.* MCC	1815
24	Players *v.* Gentlemen	1829
24	MCC *v.* Oxford University	1846
24	Hampshire *v.* MCC	1878
25	Sussex *v.* MCC	1843
25	Kent *v.* MCC	1879

HIGHEST FOURTH INNINGS TOTAL

507-7	Cambridge *v.* MCC	won	1896
502-8	Players *v.* Gentlemen	won	1900
460	Surrey *v.* MCC	lost by 5 runs	1938
412-4	I Zingari *v.* G. of England	won	1904
412-8	Gentlemen *v.* Players	won	1904
412-5	MCC *v.* Oxford	won	1904
404	MCC *v.* Cambridge	lost by 50 runs	1959

HIGHEST MATCH AGGREGATES

1603 for 28	England	653-4 dec. and 272-4 dec.	
	India	454 and 224	1990 (1)
1601 for 29	England	425 and 375	
	Australia	729-6 dec. and 72-3	1930 (2)
1502 for 28	MCC	392 and 426-4 dec.	
	N Zealand	460 and 224-4	1927
1443 for 34	Glos	478 and 243-7 dec.	
	Middlesex	478 and 244-7	1938
1406 for 36	England	487 and 301-6 dec.	
	India	221 and 397	2002 (1)
1401 for 24	Sri Lanka	555-8 dec. and 42-1	
	England	275 and 529-5 dec.	2002 (1)

FOUR INDIVIDUAL 100S IN AN INNINGS

4	543-4 dec.	Middlesex *v.* Sussex	1920
4	502-7 dec.	Middlesex *v.* Warwickshire	2001

SIX INDIVIDUAL 50S IN A MATCH

6	583-7 dec.	MCC *v.* Oxford University	1896
6	438	Middlesex *v.* Kent	1900
6	539-9 dec.	Kent *v.* Middlesex	1928
6	577	Middlesex *v.* Sussex	1938

LARGEST MARGIN OF VICTORY

427 runs	Sussex 292 and 445	
	Epsom 204 and 106	1817
417 runs	MCC 473 and 108	
	Norfolk 92 and 72	1820
409 runs	Australia 350 and 460-7 dec.	
	England 215 and 186	1948 (2)

WINS AFTER FOLLOWING ON

MCC	89 and 207	Cambridgeshire 195 and 57	1863
MCC	108 and 276	England 219 and 113	1881
Middlesex 139 and 311		Lancashire 266 and 111	1890
Middlesex 96 and 233		Notts 196 and 84	1891
Middlesex 108 and 377		Surrey 287 and 119	1893
MCC	266 and 335	Sussex 418 and 137	1897

TIED MATCHES

Oxford and Cambridge Universities	115 and 61	
MCC	69 and 107	1839
Middlesex	272 and 225	
South Africans	287 and 210	1904
MCC	371 and 69	
Leicestershire	239 and 201	1907

CHRONOLOGY

1787	Thomas Lord opens the first ground at Dorset Fields. Marylebone Cricket Club formed.	**1906**	First press box built.
1805	First Eton *v.* Harrow match.	**1909**	Imperial Cricket Conference inaugurated by England, Australia and South Africa.
1806	First Gentleman *v.* Players match.	**1923**	W.G. Grace Memorial Gates erected (Architect: Sir Herbert Baker).
1811	MCC moves to North Bank, Regent's Park.		
1814	Lord's ground moves to present site.	**1926**	Second Grandstand completed (Architect: Sir Herbert Baker). Father Time weathervane presented.
1825	William Ward buys ground lease.		
1827	First Oxford *v.* Cambridge match.		
1832	Thomas Lord dies at West Meon.	**1934**	Harris Memorial Garden created. 'Q' Stand built (Architect: Sir Herbert Baker).
1835	Lease transferred to J.H. Dark.		
1837	Jubilee match, North *v.* South.	**1937**	Car park made on practice ground.
1838	Real tennis court built (site of Mound Stand).	**1938**	First televised Test match, England *v.* Australia.
1846	First telegraph scoreboard installed.	**1949**	26 retired professional cricketers who played for England made Honorary Cricket Members of MCC.
1848	First printing tent erected; match cards sold.		
1864	First groundsman engaged.		
1865	Pavilion enlarged.	**1953**	HRH The Duke of Edinburgh opens the MCC Museum (Architect: J.H. Markham). Coronation Garden created.
1866	Ground purchased for £18,333 6s 8d.		
1866–7	First Grandstand erected (Architect: Arthur Allom).		
1867–8	Second Tavern built (Architect: Edward Paraire).	**1958**	Warner Stand opens.
		1962	Last Gentlemen *v.* Players match.
1877	Middlesex CCC first play at Lord's.	**1963**	First Gillette Cup final: Sussex beat Worcs.
1884	First Test match at Lord's.		
1887	Henderson Nursery purchased.	**1967**	New Tavern opens (Architect: David Hodges).
1888	Bill to take over the ground for railway rejected.	**1968**	Tavern Stand opens (Architect: Kenneth Peacock).
1889-90	Present pavilion built under Nursery End.		
1898	Board of Control for home Test matches first meets at Lord's.	**1969**	First meeting of the Cricket Council (MCC, TCCB and NCA).
1898-9	Mound Stand built. Tennis court built behind the pavilion.	**1972**	First Benson & Hedges Cup final: Leicestershire beat Yorkshire.
		1975	First Prudential World Cup final: West Indies beat Australia.
1902	Easter coaching classes begin.		
1904	Advisory County Cricket Committee first meet at Lord's.	**1977**	MCC Indoor Cricket School opens.
		1985	New MCC Library opens.

1986 Building of new Mound Stand (Architect: Michael Hopkins & Partners).

1987 Bicentenary of MCC: MCC *v.* the Rest of World match.
New Mound Stand opened by HRH The Duke of Edinburgh.
Bicentenary Gates presented by Duke of Westminster.

1988 Electric scoreboard installed.

1989 'Q' Stand renamed the Allen Stand.

1990 Launch of the Tour of Lord's.

1991 Opening of Compton and Edrich Stands (Architect: Michael Hopkins & Partners).

1993 Re-opening of refurbished MCC Museum.

1995 New Indoor Cricket School opens (Architect: David Morley).

1997 England & Wales Cricket Board formed.
MCC and ECB launch website on the internet.

1998 Third Grandstand opened (Architect: Nicholas Grimshaw & Partners).
Brian Johnston Film Theatre opened in MCC Museum.
First women members of MCC are admitted.
W.G. Grace 150th anniversary match: MCC *v.* the Rest of the World (in aid of the Diana Princess of Wales Memorial Fund).

1999 Media Centre opened (Architect: Future Systems).
Electronic scoreboard installed on Allen Stand.

2000 100th Test match at Lord's: England *v.* West Indies.

2001 100th England Test match at Lord's: England *v.* Pakistan.

2003 Graham Smith scores 259 for South Africa in the Second Test at Lord's as the *v.*isitors notch up 682 for 6 declared

D.G. Cork hits F.A. Rose for 6 during the 2nd Cornhill Test, England *v.* the
West Indies at Lord's in 2000. (Photograph by Patrick Eagar.)

INDEX